Mastering the Art of Ritual Magick

Book I: Foundation

By Frater Barrabbas

Mastering the Art of Ritual Magick

Book I: Foundation

By Frater Barrabbas

Stafford, England

Megalithica Books

Mastering the Art of Ritual Magick
Frater Barrabbas
© 2008 First edition

Cover Design: Andy Bigwood
Internal Illustrations: Soror Rekhetra Qadesh and Keith Ward
Editor: Joni Strandquest
Layout: Lupa

Set in Book Antiqua and Kingthing Exeter
Kingthings font care of Kevin King, font designer,
http://mysite.wanadoo-members.co.uk/Kingthings/index.htm

Megalithica Books edition 2008
A Megalithica Books Edition
http://www.immanion-press.com
info@immanion-press.com

8 Rowley Grove
Stafford ST17 9BJ
UK

ISBN 978-1-905713-20-2

DEDICATION

This series is dedicated to:
Lady Charis Kai Aleithea,
who inspired the writing of this work so many years ago,
and taught me to always seek the ways of Light and Love.

ACKNOWLEDGEMENTS

Salute to:
Frater Kalixtus, Frater Arjuna and Frater Anubis
core members of the Order E.S.S.G.,
who believed in what I was doing more than I did.

Special thanks to:
Soror Rekhetra Qadesh and Keith Ward
for the contribution of your talents
through artwork and illustration.

Grace Victoria Swann,
for all of your help and assistance that really made
this work possible.

Table of Contents

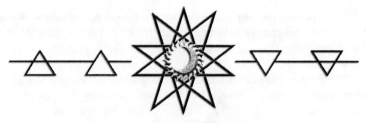

The Getting Of Gnosis

Through the kindness of a mutual friend I met Frater Barrabbas in 1986. It was our love for Western yoga (Magick) that cemented our relationship, sparked our conversations and enlivened discussions. Much of what is best within me now, I owe to the reverberation of our encounters and to the subsequent growth within my magickal life.

I noticed early on that Frater Barrabbas bore unique qualities to his magickal vision and work. He held neither derivation nor dependency upon past systems of magickal exploration in his philosophy. While within his efforts, I saw a respect for traditions of the past -- Kabbalistic, Enochian, Freemasonry, Golden Dawn, Thelemic and Neopagan -- Frater Barrabbas was not content to retrace old patterns within ritual Circle. Instead, he used them as jumping off points for deeper pioneering while in the transfigured time and space.

Eventually (albeit with great reluctance on his part and even greater prodding on my part) he allowed me to see his magickal diaries and rituals. Nothing could have prepared me for what I would see; they presented innovative ritual structures, such as the Vortex and the Elemental Octagram.

Frater Barrabbas and I shared a frustration that contemporary 20th century Magick seemed to be dedicated to endless variations on themes established in the past -- frozen in time.

We were not alone in this belief. Others of like mind came together to form the Egregora Sancta Stella Gnostica (E.S.S.G.) a gnostic ritual magick order. Uniting us was Frater Barrabbas's view that the sheer stasis of contemporary Magick was evident by the nature of the information available to the occultist in the public arena. Regardless of its historical riches, the occult tradition had essentially become a prison with its doors locked from the inside.

Drawing his imagination, inspiration and intuition from Western esotericism, Frater Barrabbas' view of the Magickal world hinges on Valentinian Gnosticism. Gnosis is the eternal mantram of Neti Neti Atma, and the vanguard against orthodoxy.

The very nature of the Gnostic experience through Magickal technique and rite must be truly free; dependent upon no tradition save for the spiritual/mental constructs of the magician themselves.

Mastering the Art of Ritual Magick series presents all three areas of lore involved in the practice of ritual into a single system of magick: the background knowledge, the Grimoire of rituals and the Key of creative adaptation. The final element makes for a unique contribution to the literature of magick.

Frater Barrabbas declares the magician to be an artist, thus this book is your palette for allowing every idea to become an ideal, which creates vital forces within to transform consciousness. The path of magick as described in these pages goes beyond the well known definitions of what magick is. Rather it demonstrates the magician's symbolic role in the cosmogonic processes of creation, dissolution and remembering. This is the dance of Shiva, the myth of Isis and Osiris, the descent of Orpheus, the crucifixion of Odin, the forging of the Sampo and the quest for the Grail.

Another point of interest are the magickal diary entries of Frater Anubis. They provide insight into the actual workings of the E.S.S.G., offering innovation based on group consensus rather than central authority from any entity, discarnate or otherwise. There is also a discussion on the ethics of esoteric group work, which provides current and future E.S.S.G. lodges with two unique qualities rare in similar group efforts - creative freedom and duration.

For Frater Barrabbas, the ceremonial magickian is bound inexorably to dogma, creed, and doctrine. The ritual magickian has never forgotten their stellar origins and shamanic roots in the true alchemical marriage of Earth, Self and Space.

The methods in this book invite the ritual magickian to transform consciousness beyond the boundaries of this world. To realize (that) the boundary of the noumenon has no boundary at all. This is a new Grimoire for a New Age for the magickal explorer willing to seek out "love, which moves the sun and the other stars."[1]

Frater Kalixtus
(Beltane, 1996)

---

1 *The Divine Comedy* - Hell - Canto XXXIII by Dante Alighieri

Foreword

It's been more than a decade since I first wrote the *Mastering the Art of Ritual Magick* series (initially titled the Pyramid of Powers). Ten years ago the contents that make up this book were deemed unacceptable and rejected by publishers because it was "too advanced" for occult audiences of the time.

Much has changed in the world since the time. Back in those days global events seemed to indicate that the world was maturing and that the old order was quietly passing away into history, preparing the way for a more enlightened era.

But as we crossed into the new millennium, we emerged into a dark and nightmarish world. As I write these words, traditions of the past are warring with the ideals of the future. The world is grappling with terrorists and religious fanatics who espouse a singular medieval mind set.

We, in America, have hardly experienced the new global order that the world seemed on the threshold of becoming ten years ago. Instead, the world that we have come to know has been altered by the numbers for the date, September 11th, or 9/11.

Many things seem irrelevant that were said and done before that date. But the passing of time has not made this work less relevant; in fact, I believe it is more relevant now than it ever was before.

Ritual magick is still the preeminent methodology in the West for gaining enlightenment, and that has not changed in the decade since this book was first written. What has changed is that there are more individuals who need to develop their own magickal system, independent of other various occult organizations or magickal orders. This book was developed and written to satisfy that need, and now it has finally found its way into print, ready to launch a new generation of ritual magicians into the more positive pursuits of spiritual autonomy and self direction.

Some of the information presented in this work has never been presented to occultists, and it will be interesting to see how they receive it and what ultimately is done with it. This work certainly sets the stage for the presentation of more advanced material, and in that vein I may publish some of the collected lore of the Order of the Gnostic Star, and bring to the occultists of the Western Mystery tradition the methodologies of elemental and talismanic magick.

Frater Barrabbas Tiresius
- A Disciple of Magick
Autumn Equinox 2007

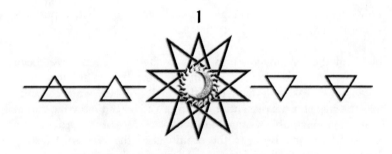

Introduction

We begin this book, *Mastering the Art of Ritual Magick*, with an important objective -- to advance our knowledge of ritual magick and its occult underpinnings.

It's assumed that you, the student magician, have already established some level of ritual practice, ideally the practices proposed in the book *The Disciple's Guide to Ritual Magick*, and that you have become competent, experienced, and comfortable in that practice. However, there much more to the study and practice of ritual magick than what was written in my previous book. That work was just an introduction, a means of getting a student to approach magick as a comprehensive discipline.

The next step for a magician is to write his or her own personal magickal system, combining all of the studies, insights and experiments into a completely new formulation. Why is this important as a next required step in the development of a ritual magician? First, successfully writing a magickal system will give you a wealth of knowledge and experience. Second, you, the magician, must use a magickal system that is intimately meaningful and produces profound and life changing experiences for you. Just utilizing other people's rituals, and perhaps mutating them or just using them as is will not gain the earth shaking transformations and powerful insights that are *de rigueur* of the experienced ritual magician.

The challenge is to write from scratch a complete system of ritual magick. The reason for this challenge should be obvious – to make it your own system. No longer can you just accept the word of other people, even if they are considered wise and masterly.

You must leave the popular path of practicing simple rites and acquiring lore from books or the internet, and instead forge a completely new system of ritual magick. However, as your writer and teacher, I won't just throw you to the wolves by telling you to have at it without any assistance or a plan. We will work together, you and I, and examine this advanced lore. Our objective is to understand ritual magick from a much deeper and insightful level – to know and understand how ritual magick works so well that we can easily write our own rituals, or intelligently examine other people's rituals.

Ritual magicians seek to know and define the world of Spirit, and don't rely on the conjectures of others to realize this search. They are insular and generally aloof from social organizations, and they experiment and attempt to push the envelope of their knowledge. This is because they are seekers, and seekers aren't ever satisfied with either their accomplishments or their experientially based knowledge. There is always more to learn, new insights to develop, research to perform, avenues to explore, and new lore to master. Ritual magicians continue to work and perfect their art far beyond what most people accept as "spiritual" in traditional churches or religious organizations.

Ritual magicians start out their journey seeking power over themselves and their circumstances. They develop and experiment with rituals that will gain them an edge in the world that they struggle to master. They make mistakes, learn from them (hopefully), and evolve their thinking and the lore that they practice over time. Experience accumulates over the years, and what magicians practice as ritual magick changes over time as well. Their rituals start out attempting to gain money and good fortune, but always seem to end up just seeking for greater spiritual knowledge. However, there is no ancient, eternal, and therefore static knowledge waiting out there somewhere to be discovered. Knowledge is a dynamic thing, especially spiritual knowledge. It is assumed that if magicians persist in their magick that they will ultimate achieve their greatest task, union with the Godhead. They certainly didn't start out with that as their objective, and oddly, the magick that they worked led them on from one objective to another, until they managed to master themselves and their life situation, at least to the point where they found *a great solace in their work and accomplishments.* That is the larger task that magicians seek to achieve, and it is the state of mind that necessarily exists just prior to the achievement of at-one-ment with the Godhead.

Our present objective is much more humble and down to earth than achieving spiritual union. We want to be able to perform magick as a process of continual transformation and self-discovery. Achieving this task will allow us to learn to master our lives, and ourselves and so prepare us for the acquisition of spiritual knowledge that will become a great wisdom – one that we can apply to others and ourselves as well.

Popular culture has tossed around the phrase "Learn to think outside the box" so much that it has lost its meaning. It seems to say, "forget what you know and learn to think differently." I think that there is an important consideration one should ponder before learning to think "outside the box." I always thought it amusing that so many pundits were telling people to think outside the box when they had not really completed their understanding of what was in the box in the first place. The challenge I am giving to you is to write a new magickal system that requires you to think outside of the box; but this work needs to define the structures of that box carefully, so we can be certain that we know what's in the box before moving outside of it. *This present work is dedicated to carefully determining the nature of ritual magick so we can later proceed beyond it, and write a brand new system of ritual magick.*

This brings us to the subject at hand – the present work. There are nine topics that we seek to understand in greater detail so as to prepare us for the work of building a new personalized system of ritual. These nine topics are fully covered in this book, and they are arranged as the different sections in this work.

* Divine Tetrad
* Magickal Power
* Magickal Persona
* Mind Control
* Sacred Space
* Ritual Structures
* Ritual Performance
* Transformative Initiation
* Mysteries

Our objective is to cover in greater detail these nine topics, one for each of the succeeding sections of this book. If we complete this objective, then we will have the accumulated lore and information needed to proceed to the next task, which will be building a new and personalized system of magick. But let us examine each of these topics and see what it is that we will seek to learn in this work.

The Four Elements of the Magician

The very beginning of magickal knowledge concerns itself with the four Elements and the concept of the Divine Tetrad. This basic structure is used throughout magickal systems in the Western Mystery tradition. I will expound on the symbolism of the four Elements and their correspondences, an understanding which is essential to the practice of more advanced magick.

Magickal Concepts of Power

A further and deeper definition of magickal power and the mechanisms of ecstasy and applied energy will be explained to assist you to tap into magickal powers and use them in ritual magick. We will explore the metaphor of magickal power and spirit. The positive effects produced by these forces and entities represent their responsible and ethical use. Elemental sacraments will also be revealed as the physical representations of magickal power. In future phases of study, you will be required to build your own rituals of empowerment, so understanding this topic was essential.

The Magickal Identity

This section will give you detailed instructions for the development of the magickal image of the self through the magickal identity, magickal name and the magickal motto. Development of the magickal persona assists in the development of your sense of self, giving you the self-mastery that ultimately triggers the process of continuous spiritual evolution. The transformation of the mundane person into a spiritual being of light is the quest for those practicing radical and progressive magick. The magickal persona must be so empowered and integral to you and your work that it becomes second nature. As part of this, you must also develop the means to begin to approach dedicating yourself to the practice and mastery of ritual magick.

Techniques of Mind Control

The most basic discipline in the art of ritual magick is the control of one's own mind through the use of various yogic techniques. Mind-control allows you to experience altered states of consciousness, a state critical to the successful performance of magick. This form of magickal yoga consists of advanced methods of breath control, mantra and yantra meditation, concentration and contemplation. We will also cover deeper methods of self-hypnosis, suggestion (linguistic programming), and other forms of trance. In addition, some of the methods proposed by Franz Bardon will also be explored, since they represent true intermediate practices.

Magickal Topology (Sacred Space)

The world of the magician consists of the seven worlds of occult reality known as the Seven Planes. These Seven Planes represent the domain of the Inner Planes, the *cyberspace* of magick. The magician also acknowledges a conceptual division between the Macrocosm (the God-level) and the Microcosm (the individual). The representation of this dual state symbolizes the process of magick as the polarity of God and humanity. However, its ultimate goal is found in the union of Deity and humankind. This is the Unified Field Theory of Spirituality, and it is the foundation upon which all magickal operations are based.

There is also a description of the symbolic reality of the magician as realized in the domain of the magick temple or grove, the Macrocosm superimposed upon the Microcosm of the magician. We will also examine the nature of the Inner Planes, the place where spirits reside and magick is generated. All of the parts of this alternate reality will be explored and explained to reveal their symbolic significance in the scheme of ritual magick.

Magickal Ritual Structures

The specific geometric symbols (devices) of ritual magick and their use as talismanic images represent the core of the art of magick. These items have been presented in various books and documents on ritual magick, but not in the context of their use in a ritual working. We will examine the magickal devices of the Spiral, the

Hexagram , the mudras (body gestures) and asanas (postures). Methods of visualization and their uses in ritual will also be presented, as well as the basic ritual structures of the midpoint, pylon, pyramid, sphere and spiral.

The Performance of Ritual

Actions and expressions associated with the performance of ritual consist of the utterance of words of power, circumambulations, drawing lines of force, drawing symbolic devices and structures and techniques of ecstatic dance.

The master pattern of ritual workings was already presented to you in the previous work, that is, the progression of the seven steps of self, space, power, alignment, intention, objective and insight, representing the seven steps of ritual magick from the inner self to the outer world. We will cover derivations of this master pattern including the definition of the four types of workings and the use of the Gate to modify them.

The three mysteries of the Moon, Sun, and Initiation will also be briefly defined. All of these ritual steps assist you in applying personal power and meaning to successfully cause internal and external changes.

Transformative Initiation

The most significant item, perhaps in the whole book, is the Cycle of Initiation and how it profoundly transforms the male or female spiritual seeker. The twenty-two stages of the Cycle of the Hero are translated into a format capable of being ritually enacted, thus establishing the basis for the feminine and the masculine mysteries of the self in transformation. There is another use of the initiation cycle that is also presented in this section, which are the six steps of introspection or *psychic tracking*. The internal psychological dialogue with one's inner self is thus explained in detail. This method of psychic tracking uses the initiation cycle for self-actualization.

Five Mysteries

The performance of rituals and undergoing initiation has a context, and that context is found in the Mysteries. We will explore the five mysteries as they pertain to the ritual magician practicing a form of earth-based spirituality. These represent the whole of the experience of magicians, and that is, everything that they either can or will experience in their lifetimes and perhaps, even beyond. The five mysteries are found in the specific rituals that celebrate the cycles of the Moon, Sun and the Self – all of which are in constant motion and change. We will also cover the paradoxical nature of the Deity, and that it may be represented as one Deity, two, many, or even as symbolic archetypes, and still, the truth will not be fully realized. The mysteries are real, and can only be approached through immersion and direct experience.

Now that we have revealed our objective in the nine sections stated above, let us begin our work together, and seek to master this important lore so we can arrive at the place where the real work begins.

I promise in this undertaking that you will discover all sorts of new ideas and information. These will help you gain a greater in-depth knowledge of some topics that you already thought you knew.

You are invited to begin this journey with me, and together we will attempt to determine what is really "inside the box."

So, let us begin...

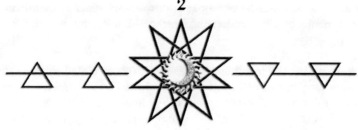

2

The Four Elements of the Magician

Introduction: The Pyramid's Base

The most basic structure associated with the study of ritual magick in the Western Magickal tradition is found in the tetrad.

The tetrad occurs within all symbolic correspondences and is usually associated with the four Elements. Since many comparable symbolic structures in the Western occult tradition are related to the four Elements, they act as the base to all workings of magick. This is why I call it the "Pyramid's base". It is the platform upon which all magickal operations are built.

The four Elements have a large number of correspondences in ritual magick including the four Quarters of the magick circle and the four elemental tools. They reveal the essential components of ritual magick and are represented as magickal formulas, typically in the form of acronyms.

The tetrad corresponds to various sacred four-letter words (the tetragrammatons of YHVH, I.N.R.I., AGLA, etc.) known throughout the disciplines of Western religion and occultism.[2]

As a formula, the tetrad represents the four cosmic stages of creation, preservation, regeneration and dissolution. These four stages are symbolized by the eternal cycle of being, wherein the processes of creation and transformation occur through the agency of magick. So the tetrad symbolizes and acts as a metaphor for the process of magick and its effects. This represents the inherent nature

---

[2] The most commonly known tetrad is the name of the Hebrew God, represented by the initials YHVH. This tetrad is usually pronounced Yahweh; however, Orthodox Judaism stipulates that this tetrad has no actual pronunciation.

of all magickal four-letter words of power, and specifically the four letter name of God, called the Tetragrammaton by the Hellenist Jews.

By examining the four Elements as they are articulated through the four-letter word of power (the YHVH of the Hebrews), we can then expand the definition and reveal more detailed qualities associated with the Elements. Through this simple exercise, we produce a more operational definition of the Elements, allowing them to be more readily perceived and manipulated by in magickal rituals.

2.2 The Tetrad of YHVH

The Tetragrammaton

The four Elements, and therefore, the Tetrad, are subjects that have already been covered in my previous book *The Disciple's Guide to Ritual Magick*[3]. Therefore, we will consider more intermediate coverage of these topics from this point on.

The following are some important points that define the divine tetrad in greater detail.

The Tetrad:

- Is a symbolic structure representing the extension of being expressed in the full spectrum of life from the most abstract and symbolic level to the most physically inert.
- Represents the power that causes that which is possible to become manifest through the progression of idea to form.
- Consists of the four archetypal Elements of Fire, Water, Air and Earth.
- Is a magickal word of power, and when correctly uttered may cause unlimited possibilities for creation and transformation.
- Symbolizes the resolution of the trinity; the transformation of idea (as the number 3 represents) into form (as represented by the number 4).

The qualities of the tetrad represent the manifestation of all that is - the Deity in the act of creation. It can also be viewed as a

---

[3] See Frater Barrabbas – *Disciple's Guide to Ritual Magick*, pp. 122 - 125

progression of stages representing spiritual evolution. This may be described as a twofold process consisting of ascension and incarnation .

Ascension is the process where seekers realize the godhead within themselves. Incarnation, or creation, is a process where the Deity seeks to immerse its spiritual essence into the diversity of manifested life.

Analyzing each letter in the tetrad of YHVH serves to define the whole formula in greater detail. We must also keep in mind the fact that there are various other examples of the divine tetrad found in many different cultures and languages, whose letters are different but basic meaning is analogous.

2.2.1 The Letter Yod as Fire

The first letter is Yod, which signifies divine Fire, conceived in the image of a lightening bolt or an all-consuming fire. Yod is electric, expansive and volatile. It is the primal creative power that is both swift and violent in its expression. It also symbolizes the archetype of masculinity, particularly, as the spermatozoon. Yod is unbounded and consists of pure intellect.

The first stage of creation is the conception of form as an idea or thought, and therefore Yod symbolizes primordial thought. It is not yet individuated, so it represents the initial state of awareness known as the dawn of consciousness. This is symbolized by the archetype of the Universal Mind, preceding all material things.

The letter Yod also represents the world of Atziluth of the Qabbalists. In this place dwell the symbolic archetypes of Spirit; the mind of the Godhead resides in its core. When working magick, the magician must first engage this archetypal world and its creative powers in order to contemplate transforming the material world.

2.2.2 The First Letter Heh as Water

The second letter is Heh, which represents the feminine receptor of the divine fire (as Yod). It's the foundation upon which the pure symbolism of Yod is given meaning, significance and value. It functions like a fertilized ovum in the cosmic womb. The origin of consciousness consists of a myriad of archetypes existing as pure ideals; but they only become intelligible when they interrelate with each other and form patterns of meaning. The feminine aspect of Heh causes this formation of relationships between autonomous ideals, and so thoughts and ideas, as the aggregate of ideals, forms. In this manner, symbols acquire meaning.

The evaluation of an abstract ideal gives it a meaning and significance that it might not otherwise possess. Pure symbolism has no intrinsic meaningfulness. Symbols gain their meaning through an analysis and a determination of content, contrast and context. These are all qualities that Heh gives to the domain of perfect ideals.

Heh symbolizes the archetypal female, therefore, it polarizes the qualities of the letter Yod, posing as its equal opposite. Heh is magnetic, contractile, and stable. Through Heh, the intense energies of creation are given form and substance, becoming stabilized and intelligible; that is, they are given meaning. This is the creative process whereby the super symbolic World of the Absolute is given significance, and where its various ideals are ordered and given individual values and meaningfulness. The significance of creating new meaning through ordering imparts realization and inner certainty (truth), which combine to empower, project and illuminate the Universal Mind.

The primary energy that emerges at this stage of creation, where the archetypal masculine and feminine unite, is love in its purest fullest expression, the greatest power of all powers. It is only in the Element of Earth and its illusory fall from spiritual grace that one finds the second and opposing power, which is fear. Fear is the opposite of love, and the source of hatred, violence, and destruction. Fear is essentially based upon illusion, but a very dangerous illusion indeed.

2.2.3 The Letter Vav as Air

The third letter is Vav, which symbolizes the union of the primal pair (the Yod and Heh) and also the process of mediation.

Vav represents the laws dictating the pattern of being and the beginning stage of the ordering of conscious reality. The key word applied to this state of consciousness is synthesis. The merging and union of the archetypal male and female creates the offspring that is the group-mind (egregore), which represents the primal mediator of all opposites.

It also represents the power of the individual will and the first definition of individuality, which occurs before material manifestation. This stage of creation represents the world of individual minds, thoughts, and their domain, which is always

subtly influenced by the convergence of the archetypal and symbolic levels of being. Individuals are rarely aware of the source of all individuality. Only when there is an absence of all physical distraction do they become aware of this source of individuality and have access to its more abstract levels of being.

The Qabbalists referred to this world as the World of Formation, or Yetzirah. It is here where higher minds may commune with the Absolute Spirit. Individual spirits can manifest as angels, daemons, nature spirits, or ancestral human beings. Yet even though all of these spiritual emissaries appear to be beings of disembodied consciousness that act as individuals, their sense of uniqueness is only a mask through which the Absolute Spirit may observe or act.

The word formation used to describe this world refers to the masks of appearance that give structure and order to the mental world, and this is another quality of Vav. However, the world of the mind is extremely volatile and even illusory. Although limited by knowledge and experience in the temporal world, the mind can project beyond its limitations through the imagination, and is therefore truly without bounds.

2.2.4 The Final Letter Heh as Earth

The fourth letter of the tetrad is the letter Heh final, which represents not only a recurrence but also a final solidification of the feminine forces. It is the creator of all physical life, the author of the physical world as the great Earth Mother who is also the daughter and beloved of the Absolute Spirit. And like lovers, the physical and spiritual worlds merge to produce a  harmonious combination or synthesis of both. The Spirit amidst physical manifestation is the synergy of animated existence that is constantly evolving within the entropic universe.

The true essence of the final Heh is revealed in the pristine state of nature, which is the pure model or ideal of the physical world. It is also the realization of the spark of spirit in all things endowed with physical life.

The Qabbalists ascribe to the final solidification of spirit in matter the world of Assiah. One of its particular attributes is the existence of good and evil and their spiritual personifications as the Lord of Light and the Lord of Darkness, or the Devil. That which is considered good is accepted and sought after, and conversely, that which is evil is rejected and shunned. But even in this state of division exists the transforming agent of spiritual union, the power of physical love. When people cease from conflict and the affects of division pass, then the natural state of peaceful cooperation ensues as the power of love grows.

There are many definitions of the word love, indicating various levels of human consolidations, but they describe a similar phenomenon - the drawing together of people into ever-larger social organizations. This harmonious union represents the archetype of the ideal world-order towards which humans are ever striving. This archetypal world is utopian, and can be represented by the primordial Garden of Eden, or by an Atlantis of the future.

A utopia, by definition, is always unobtainable; but it is also revered and held up as a brilliant ideal, like the shining city on the hill or the fabled castle of Camelot. Therefore, the ultimate goal of the synergy of spirit animating life is the fusion of all life into a single conscious being. This is the ultimate evolutionary realization for all living beings. It is the original place where the Absolute Spirit began the process of creation itself, and therein was divided into a multitude of sentient beings, all for the purpose of this destiny of spiritual union.

2.3 The Four Elemental Tools and Spirit

Magickal tools are used in ritual and ceremonial magick to amplify and project the powers of the elements as well as perform other tasks. If we use the Greater Key of Solomon as a typical source of magickal tools, we will find a white and black hilted knife, a dagger, scimitar, sickle, poniard, burin, staff, and wand, as well as a sword. Planetary talismans and the lamen (pentacle or seal of Solomon) rounded out the repertoire of the classical Solomonic magician. Then there was also the temple furniture, burning incense, an inscribed magic circle, various vestments, jewelry, and other accouterments particular to the practice of ceremonial magick.

In Solomonic magick, each of these tools had very specific uses, and each was specially consecrated and engraved with magickal sigils and Hebrew letters. This regimen of magickal tools varied from grimoire to grimoire. There were similarities but no accepted standard. Magickal tools were purely operational and used for very specific purposes in ritual, and had no additional symbolic meaning or associations. Curiously enough, a list of tools prior to the late 19th century didn't include any kind of cup or dish. These would have been identified as Christian and associated with the Catholic Mass.[4]

The incorporation of the Tarot into Western Occultism caused the Elements to become associated with the tools. The Tarot was examined and given Qabbalistic attributes, and the systems of ceremonial magick were influenced by that association and organized in a fashion not previously known. The four suits of the Tarot became the symbolic analogues for the Four Elements, which were also associated with the Divine Tetrad. The four suits became, by analogy, four magickal tools, as presented in the teachings of the Golden Dawn. This association of Element with symbolic Tarot Suit and magickal tool produced two different schools. However, it was the Golden Dawn who simplified the diverse collection of magickal tools, organizing them with the Tarot. This was a new perspective as conceived within the Golden Dawn, which had no prior exemplar.

If we examine occult writings prior to the Golden Dawn, we will find no reference to the elemental association of the four magickal tools. It is certainly not found in Agrippa's classic *Occult Philosophy* or in the early 19th century variation called *The Magus*.

It is first discovered in the writings of the late nineteenth and early twentieth century. These were works that expounded on the subject of the Occultic and Qabbalistic associations of the Tarot. It is here where the association is made between the four elements and the attributes of the four Tarot Suits. The writings of Eliphas Levi and S. L. Mathers appear to be the first to make this association and then it is further and more solidly made by Papus in his book *Tarot of the Bohemians* (1896).

This idea was either picked up or simultaneously derived at approximately the same time in the teachings and rituals of the Golden Dawn.[5] However, the association of Suit and Element is rectified and laid out in a constructive fashion by Papus in his later book.

A. E. Waite's book, *The Pictorial Guide of the Tarot* (1911) does not make this association, but is well established in another work,

---

[4] This statement is not exactly correct - some versions of the Key of Solomon use a cup to catch the blood of the victim. But the Chalice as an important magickal and sacramental tool was not part of that lore.

[5] The association of the Tarot suits to common playing card suits first appears in a work written by Mathers, but it is poorly contrived.

The General Book of the Tarot, written by Dr. A.E. Thierens[6], which contains a written introduction by Waite. In that book the correspondences between Astrology and the Tarot were developed, particularly in regards to the four Suits and the minor Arcana.

Using the Qabbalah or Astrology to determine the elemental attributes of the four suits of the Tarot produces two different sets of associations. When the Qabbalah is used, the order of elements begins with Fire, then Water, Air and finally, Earth. When one uses Astrology with Theosophic influences, the elements begin with Air, and proceed to Water, Fire, and Earth. The order of the four Suits of the Tarot does not change, and begins with Wands or Scepters (Clubs), Cups (Hearts), Swords (Spades) and finally, Coins or Pentacles (Diamonds). The sequence denotes the hierarchy associated with the four levels of the European social order of nobility, clergy, military (land owners) and merchants (artisans).

The elemental associations for these four suits differs whether Wands are considered to be Fire and Swords are Air, as in the Qabbalistic system, or whether Wands are considered Air and Swords, Fire, as in the Astrological system. These two approaches have produced two different sets of associations, and spawned two different systems of magick, as far as the four elemental tools of magick are concerned. Both systems are substantiated by symbolic correspondences, and either will work quite well. What is required is for the magician to adhere to either one or the other, depending on what makes sense and works for the individual.

The four tools have the elemental configuration of the Wand, which is Fire or Air, the Cup or chalice, which is Water, the Sword, which is Air or Fire, and the Pentacle or Dish (paten), which is Earth. All tools that the magician uses to project magickal power are a variation of these four Elemental Tools. In order to understand the significance and use of these tools, it is important to examine the symbolic correspondences and variations for each tool, and how they qualify the association of the Element with that tool.

The Wand and the Staff

The wand is a tool that is used to summon, draw down or seal the magickal power or associated spirits. It is a symbol of the divine rod that transmits and receives the powers and spiritual intelligence of the Universal Mind through the mind of the magician.

---

[6] Dr. Thierens was a renowned Dutch astrologer and Theosophist.

The archetypal wand is double terminated, meaning that both ends of the rod are can be used to both project and receive power, since it is a symbolic conduit between the material world and World of Spirit.

This tool is the exemplar of the winged wand with entwined twin snakes (the Caduceus) used by the god Mercury (Hermes) to heal and reveal the will of the gods. It is therefore an instrument that determines fate and fortune, and communicates the intuitive wisdom (Gnosis) of the gods within the domain of Spirit. When using it, the magician is emulating the Godhead in the acts of creation, restoration (preservation) and destruction.

A subtle instrument with a multitude of uses, the wand can take a variety of forms. Typically, it is as long as the magician's fore-arm, and is measured from the palm to the elbow, being therefore, an extension of the magician's hand. It is fashioned from the branch of a tree, and the wood that is used is as significant as its shape and adornment. The double wand is like the Divine Yod, or Lightening Bolt, it is multi-directional (simultaneously sending and receiving) and is used to project the greater and deeper powers of the magician acting as the Deity.

However, if it has only one end, then it obscures the receiving capability and favors its projecting capability (but it can do both). A single terminated wand may be phallic shaped (the better to create), tipped with a pinecone or a crystal. A single terminated wand with a phallic tip is an obvious representation of the masculine creative power, representing that the magician has the ability to create as both an agent of the masculine and feminine forces. The wand is a fetish symbolizing the magician's power and fertility.

If the wand is interpreted as being of the element of Air, then it represents the Logos, the projected ideal that the magician uses to create, and has both the emphasis of the word of power and the projection of the Wand as an instrument of the Divine Will. If it's interpreted as being of Fire, then it represents the Illumination of Divine Wisdom, the means by which the mind and soul of the magician is inspired and enlightened by the higher self, or God/dess Within.

A crystal terminated wand is called a transmutar wand. It's used in combination as both a dagger and a wand, so it is considered a hybrid. The transmutar wand is typically used in conjunction with a base crystal (found in the center of the magick circle or on the altar) and a control crystal (worn around the magician's neck). It represents one of the three components of a specific form of high magick that uses crystals to store and project magickal powers, ritual constructs and spiritual intelligences.

The wand is used to draw the four spirals that invoke, banish, seal and unseal, and these spirals project the power in a specific manner, creating a spell that opens and closes gateways between the worlds. The wand is therefore the primary tool that the magician uses to establish a link between worlds, channeling powers and spiritual contacts through the mystical gateway of higher consciousness. It is this reason that the tool most associated with the magician is the magick wand, and that all of the other tools seem quite obscure in comparison.

Another analogue of the wand is the staff, which is a larger and more extended version of the wand. The powers and qualities of the staff are the same as the wand, but only greater. The staff has some uses that the wand, owing to its size, does not. While the wand is a personal tool and is generally not shared with others, the staff is large enough to be used by several practitioners together in order to raise magickal energy.

The staff signifies authority and seniority (like the crosier), denoting that the owner is a spiritual leader as well as the proper representative of the Deity. The staff is an obvious conduit for a spirit to manifest and for matter to ascend into spirit, traveling up or down, from the nadir to the zenith and back again. The staff is an analogue for the Cosmic Pole, Stang or World Tree, and so it stands erected between worlds, representing the primary symbolic marker representing the World of the Spirit and its inhabitants, bridging both worlds together and drawing them into a single world - the central domain magicians and their magick circle.

The Cup or Chalice

The Cup or Chalice represents the Element of Water; it is a representation of the feminine magickal force. The cup is capable of holding and containing liquids, which are used as sacraments.

One of the roles of the magician is a priest/ess of the Deity, and as such, must be able to generate the basic sacraments. These consist of the lustral or holy water, sacramental wine or beer, and sacramental cakes or bread (hosts).

The chalice is used to generate the lustral water and also hold the sacramental drink. The cup as a magickal tool has an ancient precedent in the creation and dispensing of love philters -- that ancient spell of seduction, love and bonding. The basic component was the introduction of a bodily fluid, usually blood, into a drink to disguise it, and then giving it to the intended victim to unwittingly consume.

The accompanied fascination spell, auto-suggestion, and amorous coercion were part of an ancient magickal practice, and one that the magician practiced for personal gain as well as on behalf of others. The higher and more exalted use of this old and simple spell is to forge a bond between magicians and their imago of the Deity, so the reformation of this rite is the communion rituals of alignment.

The generation of lustral water is used to consecrate and bless the magick circle within the temple and create a holy or sacred space. The generation of the communion wine is used to establish a powerful bond between magicians and their Deity, thus allowing them to become one with it, and emulate its powers and wisdom. Therefore, magicians typically use at least two separate cups, one for the lustral water and the other for the communion beverage, since it would be absurd to mix the two.

The cup, like the wand, has many forms, and can be fashioned from several different materials. It can be made of metal (silver, pewter, copper, gold, bronze or brass) or made of clay, porcelain, or even glass. The cup that holds the lustral water would have to be made of a material that can withstand the corrosive effects of such a brew, and the cup that holds the wine would have to be made of a material that would not add an unpleasant after taste. The symbolic attributes of the cup are, of course, love, compassion, and emotional and spiritual fulfillment.

The analogues of the cup are the cauldron or cooking pot, and the alchemical alembic (an alchemical still). The powers and qualities of the cup are extended and amplified in the cauldron, but we can also add to its list of qualities, regeneration, rebirth, inspiration, and insight. The cauldron is used for cooking, brewing potions and also burning herbs or parchment sigils. The alembic is used to distill and extract the essence of a thing, i.e., the creation of spirits (alcohol). The cup is a tool that holds, contains and transforms what it holds, being the bearer of a liquid sacrament in its various forms.

The Sword or Dagger

The magickal Sword or Dagger represents the basic cutting or bladed tool used by the magician. While the wand points, the dagger or sword cuts. The wand draws things together but the dagger or sword makes divisions between things.

In the Key of Solomon, and in other contemporary grimoires, there are a number of magickal weapons that have a blade. However, the three bladed tools most often mentioned are the black hilted knife, the white hilted knife and the sword. As mentioned previously, there was also a dagger, a poniard, a scimitar, a sickle, burin, and other tools.

The Golden Dawn used only double bladed weapons-- the dagger and the sword. Modern Witchcraft uses a black hilted knife called an athamé and a white hilted knife called a boline; these are probably derivations of the black and white hilted knives found in the Key of Solomon.

I personally believe that a magician needs a dagger to draw the magickal lines of force as well as a sword to ward the circle, banish unwanted entities, and to draw the circle and establish the lines of force of a vortex. A magician also needs a tool to perform various tasks, such as carving wands, engraving tool handles, wax talismans and candles, trimming candles, cutting flowers, herbs, etc. These mundane tasks prepare things for magickal use, and so an engraved and separate tool could be used to assist in the preparation of magickal products.

A magician would definitely make use of a magickal dagger with a black hilt and a magickal sword, but the crafting tool is optional, since it wouldn't be necessary to engrave and consecrate a tool for mundane magickal uses when any better and specialized tool might suffice. It's really up to the magician if such a tool is warranted.

Akin to the wand, the magickal dagger is an extension of the magician's hand. The sword can be considered analogous to the dagger, only that it is greater in size and potency. If the Element associated with the magickal Sword or Dagger is Air, then these weapons symbolize the will and intellectual discipline of the magician, and the ability to judge and spiritually discriminate. If the Element is Fire, then the Sword or Dagger represents the magician's ability to inspire, project power, and dominate.

Both definitions are valid, and they don't contradict each other. There's a martial aspect to bladed weapons and this accords well with both Fire and Air, although the sign Aries (with the ruling planet Mars) is a Fire sign and the Archangel of Fire is Michael, who brandishes a flaming sword. The dagger is used to draw lines of force, pentagrams (in the air or on an object) and other star forms, and to coerce and pierce the heart of all mysteries. The dagger or sword is a focus for the more aggressive power of the magician, and so the bladed tools are also thought of as being male.

In the Key of Solomon, the white hilted knife is the primary tool and is used in all manner of operations except drawing the magick circle and coercing spirits, which is the domain of the black hilted knife. All weapons are consecrated with the blood of a specific animal and the juice of a plant during the planetary day and hour of Mercury, except the black hilted knife, which is consecrated during the planetary day and hour of Saturn. The white hilted knife can be additionally consecrated with fire if the tool is not made with one's own hand, and this is assumed for the other tools as well. So, we can see that there is a mixture of the elements of Air (Mercury), Fire (fire consecration), and Earth (Saturn).

I believe that such a combination for the elemental association of bladed weapons is quite natural, since bladed weapons are artifices that have no natural analogue, unlike the wand (a tree branch) or the cup (a gourd). Additionally, there is a tradition that the bladed tools were to be made from the metal of a meteorite, and so the component of Spirit (star metal) is also a part of their elemental essence.

The Pentacle or Dish (Patten)

The fourth elemental tool is the Pentacle (Panticle), Dish or Patten, which is used to hold and empower the sacraments of salt and cakes (hosts). Like the chalice or cup, the Pentacle is used to consecrate sacraments, most specifically, communal food. The Element associated with this tool is Earth, and the sacred dish holds the food offerings or the salt during the event of the consecration of the sacraments. The pentagram of the pentacle represents the magician's mastery of the four elements as the quintessence, or Spirit. The pentacle is also symbolic of the ground base of the magician within the sacramental earth, or the world imbued and blessed with Spirit. The sacralized world is a symbolic analogue of the world of the magician as the temple.

The Pentacle has its analogue in the magick shield and lamen. The magick shield is a regular sword shield that is inscribed or illustrated with a powerful symbol or talisman of magickal protection, and when used, shields the magician from magickal harm and all negativity.

The magick lamen is an illustration on a piece of wood representing the magician's symbolic anagram and talismanic mystery of the magician's universe. The Golden Dawn Rose Cross and the Tree of Life are two such lamen devices, and so is the hexagramic Seal of Solomon. A lamen device is used to represent the magician's view of the universe, and so functions as both a conceptual model as well as a talismanic device used in magickal workings itself.

What all of these tools representing Earth have in common is that they characterize the ground basis of the magician's magick, his/her magickal reality. The inscribed disk of the pentacle could also have been used to project the Element of Earth just like an invoking pentagram of that element. The pentagram on a disk could be used also to protect and defend the magician, acting in concert with his/her magick ring, hooded robe and other obvious weapons (sword and dagger).

The cup and patten have no corollaries in the Solomonic system of magick, since they are magically liturgical and would have no place in Hebrew magick. In that system, the rites of the temple priesthood are kept separate and distinct from the practices of magick, if they exist at all. These tools have greater importance in magickal systems where a magician is also a priest/ess, or where a priest/ess is used to sacralize material substances that are used in the magickal rites.

In my system of magick, the sacraments consist of food and drink, not blood and flesh, as was the case in the old grimoires, like the Key of Solomon. Because of the requirement for the blood of animals and the skin of a lamb, the magician's tool kit would have consisted of various blades and containers to perform the sacrifice and collect the sacramental blood and flesh. The magician would then have acted as the high priest in the Hebrew tradition and would have performed the animal sacrifices with a similar authority and gravity, although the creature sacrificed would not have been always kosher.

Temple/Grove/Mirror as Spirit

There is also a fifth tool that extends beyond the Four Elemental Tools; this tool directly represents Spirit. It can be represented by

the Temple or Grove (consecrated space), the Magick Circle or by a large consecrated Skrying Crystal (magick mirror), which is used as the collector for all the powers raised and entities contacted. The Temple or Grove as Spirit would include all of the temple furniture (sacred topology) or grove constructions (sacred geometry), and the remainder of relics, trophies, fetishes, regalia and various magickal paraphernalia. Another tool of Spirit would be the Double Pillars, or the single central Pole, Stang, or Obelisk. The Hebrew letter representing Spirit is Shin. The letter Shin is the embodiment of the emanation of the Absolute Spirit, representing the power of mediation as the Deity incarnated into humanity. Thus when the letter is joined to the tetrad, creating the pentad, the formula YHShVH (a formulaic variation of Joshua, the deliverer, also, Messiah) is formed. The addition of Spirit causes the whole tetrad to become embodied within the level of the individual, thus making one person the complete master of his/her destiny, and therefore by analogy, the destiny of the world.

Additional tools and equipment may consist of the Bell or Gong, the Thurible or Censor, consecrated cords (the cingulum), the Scourge (symbol of discipline or threat of punishment) and the Lamps of Art (candles or oil lamps). Sacramental items would include wine or beer (fruit juice), milk and honey, cakes or bread, scented oils or waters, aromatic herbal incenses and charcoal, spring water and sea salt. Temple or Grove furniture would include the central or main altar and quarter markings (smaller altars, candle sticks or torches) for the four Watchtowers and the Four Angles.

The magick circle can be implied, inscribed, drawn or painted on the floor or ground. There can be colored lights and a sound system for an indoor temple, or luminaries and musical instruments for a grove. To make sounds other than a bell or a gong, rattles, tambourines, drums of various kinds, and even string instruments, such as harps, guitars, or keyboards, mouth instruments such as flutes and horns. Decorations, arrangements and constructions further the uniqueness of the temple or grove, and represent the final touches to the place where magick is to be performed. The combination of mood music, burning incense, candle or lamp light occurring within a temple or grove powerfully affects the mind, and prepares the self for magick.

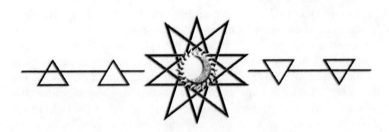

3

Ritual Structures of Magickal Power

The root of ritual magick is magickal power. It is the basis for the occurrence of psychic phenomena and the mechanism that causes psychological transformation. Magickal power, along with the inclusion of spiritual entities, represents the fundamental core of what ritual magick is and how it operates. In order to begin to master the practice of magick, one must have a good understanding of what magickal power is and how it's generated. Mastery of the techniques and engagement with spiritual entities represents the second step, which we will cover later.

In this chapter, we will demystify the myths and secrecy surrounding magickal power. It is important to have a good clear understanding of what you are doing when working ritual magick. Unambiguous definitions will help pave the way for that clarity.

3.1 A Definition of Magickal Power

Magickal power is not a term to be confused an actual quantifiable energy. It is an expression used to denote the level of intensity or resonance of a given magickal experience.

When magicians claim that a particular ritual was very powerful or that a certain series of workings were potent in their ability to cause life changes, this is not a reference to actual physical power. For instance, the energy created and experienced in a magickal ritual working could not illuminate a single electric light bulb nor be measured by any known scientific method. Since there are no measurable physical phenomena, the concept of power is metaphorical and not analogous to material power.

Magickal power refers to the level of emotional intensity and corresponding meaningfulness produced by ritual activity. There can be various subjective psychic phenomena associated with magickal rituals, some even producing physical side effects. But it is quite misleading to believe that magickal power has a basis in physical reality. The magickal phenomenon of resonance is experienced through the emotions and the physical body, denoting the level of significance and meaningfulness of a psychic event. Thus the generation of magickal power is not restricted to ritual performance alone.

The phenomena produced by magick are pervasive and also seemingly sentient, meaning that they function as an intelligent but invisible entity. This idea accords well with the concept of egregores (group-minds) and the verifiable occurrence of disembodied consciousness (ghosts and spirits). It could be conceivable that magickal power may actually be a kind of egregore, based on the theory of the unity of consciousness. However, like the homily about fish being blind to water, magicians may be unaware of the field of magick around them because it expresses itself in such a subtle and indirect manner. It is important to note that the terms power and energy represent only one perspective for classifying magickal phenomena, and they may be misleading if taken too literally.

Defined operationally as the process that causes personal transformation, magickal power is a heightened spiritual experience that the magician finds to be profoundly significant and meaningful. Rituals that can produce this effect are used by magicians to cause an intense internal change, which manifests within themselves as a continuous transformation of the psyche. While the act of assuming an altered state of consciousness functions as the ground base for perceiving magickal phenomena, it requires the addition of a symbol of transformation to act as a triggering mechanism.

The combination of an altered state of consciousness and symbols of transformation shifts perspective and allows a whole assortment of hidden powerful emotional and mental associations to become revealed. These cause a temporary change in a magician's integral self and allow the mind to experience greater transformations of the spirit, which unleash all the potentials of magickal power. The measurement of magickal power is defined as the level of intensity that one feels when undergoing an internal transformation. It can therefore be assumed that the greater the level or degree of internal transformation, the greater the degree of magickal power perceived. There is a direct correspondence between the level of emotional intensity of the magickal experience and the degree of its significance and meaningfulness to the magician.

It is also possible for individuals to share the experience of magickal power in groups, causing it to become objectified and making it real to a group as well as to the individual. The symbolic archetypes and ritual patterns employed in the generation of magickal power can impact many people simultaneously. There is a common thread of associated cultural beliefs that runs throughout magickal experiences, causing a similar type of phenomenon to occur to every individual who is exposed to it. This makes the effects of ritual magick highly uniform and capable of being communicated to numerous people, causing each of them to experience a transformation, too.

The effects of magick can be readily transmitted to others in an ever- increasing wave, described by occultists as a cascading-field effect, which ultimately can alter the sentiments of an entire cultural population. This is the reason that mainstream religions have always controlled the use of ritual (ceremonial) magick, denying its use to all but those who are members of the trained and official liturgical elite.

However, a single individual is quite capable of working magick to establish spiritual identity, and in the process, developing a personal spiritual relationship with the Deity and a magickal perspective, thereby becoming a magician in the classical definition. These changes cause a powerful sense of personal significance and direction to manifest within one's psyche, an important survival device in our digitized modern society.

When a magician is practicing ritual magick in a consistent and disciplined manner, one's personality becomes more individuated and more capable of self-mastery. This change, even if unstated, does not go unnoticed by friends, lovers, and family; even fellow workers or acquaintances notice something different. The entire social web that the magician is attached to is changed to some degree, however great or small. As the magician evolves spiritually, there is the potential of influencing others through this connection.

When individuals who have established their spiritual identity through magick join together in harmonious interaction, they add a dimension of social objectivity to their subjective pursuits, making their spiritual process collectively more real and profound. The activity of objectifying the inner self (i.e., the process of artistic expression) generates a transforming wave that ultimately can change whole social organizations and become a kind of media magick that can be absorbed as a social trend by the greater masses. This is how a dream becomes reality in our culture. The medium of this transformation is called magickal power.

One can only begin to imagine the effect that a group of well-trained magicians would have on a society, and what could be ultimately accomplished. We need only to read about the far-reaching effects that an obscure group like the Golden Dawn has had. They practiced group rituals more than a hundred years ago, then disbanded, yet what they did continues to influence the practice of modern ritual magick and esoteric religion today. The Golden Dawn was also supposed to be a secret society, because the times were such that secrecy was necessary. One must ask, how much more would such an organization have impacted the Western world if they could have had the benefit of today's tolerance and highly sophisticated electronic media, and the desire to publicly propagate their knowledge? The world awaits the coming of such a group of media magicians that will transform Western culture, bringing its people into the true realization of the Aquarian Way.

3.2 Magickal Rituals of Empowerment

The magician employs various artifices to generate magickal power and perform magickal workings. Without magickal power as the underpinning, rituals and workings become dull, meaningless activity. In fact, it is the meaningfulness of the subjective experience of magick that gives it the profound affect.

There are several theoretical approaches to describing the phenomena of magick. The energy theory is only one of them. What is being described by metaphors of power and energy is something that is more complex and intrinsic than current knowledge, both scientific and psychological, is capable of explaining.

What we can say about magickal power and its production is that it seems to function as a kind of metaphorical surrogate for sexuality, and its ultimate climax, which is ecstasy. Whatever mind-states the magician is able to derive from various physical and mental exercises, the cultivation of techniques that produce ecstatic states whenever required is an important prerequisite for the performance of ritual magick. It is also a known and documented methodology that has its roots in archaic Shamanism, and can be considered the root for the generation of all magickal power.

However, ecstasy by itself is not as impactful as ecstasy induced within a context of sacred symbology. Magick is a phenomenon where the ecstatic state is merged with meaningful and impactful symbols of transformation, producing an influx into the mind of the magician the highest states of consciousness, which are qualified by non-duality and spiritual union.

There are many mechanisms for inducing ecstasy, but there are only a few used in the practice of ritual magick. These mechanisms are referred to in the practice of ritual magick as the cone or pyramid of power, the spiral vortex, the power octagon, chanting and incantations, godhead assumption, ecstatic dance, hyperventilation (breath control), the use of sacramental substances, tools and fetishes, and sex magick itself. There are also many other mechanisms, but they represent complex variations on the basic list already given.

The first and most important consideration is that the operator of the magickal techniques of empowerment must be in a proper state of consciousness, which is a form of light trance, produced through breath control, chanting and intoning, and focused visualization. We will cover the techniques for establishing the proper magickal mind state in section 5, on Mind Control.

Another important consideration is that the space where this ritual operation is performed must be consecrated in some manner, whether that space is a temple or a grove. The work is performed within sacred space, where the atmosphere is set with candle, oil lamp or torch light, incense smoke and appropriate music. The temple or grove is decorated with symbolic structures, artwork, tools and devices; all of which are personally and profoundly meaningful to the operator. The combination of the proper mind state and the creation of sacred space together produce the potent mind altering triggers that induce the empowerment of the self.

Symbolic constructs that cause the generation of magickal power are analogous to sexual symbols, such as polarity (attraction) and union (climax). Polarity represents two opposite forces or sexual genders stimulating each other, and union is where those two opposite forces or genders are drawn together into union, causing ecstasy. It can be assumed that the greater the degree of polarity, then the greater the attraction and the greater the release within ecstasy.

The sexual polarity that's referred to in the symbols used in magick is actually variations on the archetypal masculine and the archetypal feminine. These symbols can be quite explicit or highly abstract - the effect is the same regardless. The polarity of the archetypal male and female symbolizes the psychological components involved in the process of procreation, whether that creation is internalized, such as creative and artistic inspiration, or externalized, as in the sexual creation of life.

Magick, like any of the arts, is a creative process, whether or not that which is created is tangible or intangible, physical or purely psychic. The ultimate joining occurs when the usually dormant higher conscious mind of the magician is awakened and intensely stimulated, causing it to envelope the normal conscious mind. This psychic enveloping overwhelms the usual human preoccupation with the mundane world, transporting the operator into the domain of Spirit, with its transforming effects and supernatural phenomena. Such a joining of super-consciousness with normal consciousness is all too brief, but its effects are most profound. It has produced the entire human social phenomena of religion, mysticism, occultism, spirituality and magick.

We should review the techniques of generating magickal power briefly listed above and elaborate on them, since this will expand our knowledge for producing it. The student should be aware of the fact that magickal power is produced through the analogy of the joining of sexual polarities, however they are perceived, practiced or utilized.

The Cone/Pyramid of Power (Masculine)

The cone or pyramid of power represents the symbolic masculine magickal power, and as such, it is also an analogy for the male erotic cycle. The cone of power is an obvious phallic symbol, particularly since the actual power that issues from it is like a bolt of lightning released at the moment of climax, much like the ejaculation of semen that occurs when a male achieves climax.

The basic structure of this rite is found in the analogy of the sex act from the male perspective. The continuous and ever increasing stimulation of pleasure is caused by sexual polarization

45

(i.e., the fascinated attraction of the male for the female, and the female's signaled affirmation of the masculine interest). This in turn ultimately leads to an overloading of the physical senses of touch, taste, smell and sight, culminating in the possession, dominance, and then penetration of the female by the male. An increased stimulus is achieved in the sex act itself until a plateau of sexual passion is achieved. A final intensification of stimulus produces the paroxysms of climax where the power is projected to its intended target.

How this is represented magically is in the following ritual actions. First, the focus of this type of ritual of empowerment is the polarization of the four quarters, where each archetypal masculine aspect is mated with an opposing feminine aspect. The feminine deflection of the masculine advance continues (as the erotic chase) until desire intensifies to become pure lust. This is the analogy for the circle dance, where the masculine forces pursue the feminine around the periphery of the circle.

The direction that the current of magickal power moves is deosil, spiraling from the outer periphery into the center, where the polarity of masculine and feminine meet in union. Then it moves upwards to the zenith of the circle and outwards, projecting the forces of ecstasy beyond the boundary of the magick circle.

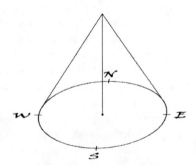

CONE OF POWER

The pyramid of power is a variation on the cone of power, with the added feature of the squaring of the circle, which is also a symbolic analogue of sexual union. The circle squared adds a greater degree of polarization and stimulation to the ritual structure. So the cone of power is the simplest method of generating power, and there are

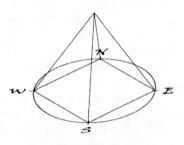

PYRAMID OF POWER

46

other more direct methods that are even more rudimentary than it.

Spiral Vortex (Feminine)

The spiral vortex represents the feminine symbolic magickal power, and it is an analogy for the female erotic cycle. The vortex has the essential qualities of being magnetic (it draws things into it) and enfolding, so its qualities very much represent the sexuality inherent in the feminine.

Polarity is not as important to this ritual structure as fusion and assimilation, although it sends out a subtle but powerful attracting magnetic force. What attracts a woman to a man is the fascination of intimately possessing and enfolding him, and she entices him in an ever increasing erotic cycle of stimulation, and powerfully draws him into her, where they both experience the fusion of sexual union. The spiral vortex uses the polarized quarters of the magick circle as merely an anchor, and

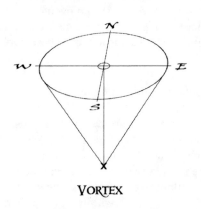

VORTEX

these are drawn together into fusion in the center of the circle.

In the female erotic cycle, there are the added metaphysical qualities of the masculine penetrating the feminine, and the feminine enfolding the masculine, producing a potential for union on at least two different levels within the woman and the man. The man may dominate the woman outwardly, but she dominates him from within, and this mutual dominance produces the powerful bond of union and its aftermath, which is sexual ecstasy. The domain where these two powers converge is within the woman's womb, and this is considered the sacred container or well of life, where the creative powers are focused.

The feminine power of a vortex spirals around the circle in a widdershins direction, fusing into union in the center and moving downwards into a subterranean singularity. The vortex holds the power within itself, just as woman harnesses the power of a man's erect penis. As the stimulus achieves a climactic crescendo, the focus of the power is pulled ever deeper into the singularity, while waves of ecstatic force emanate outwards, like the ripples produced by a pebble dropped into a pond or the tsunami produced by oceanic earthquakes.

The emanating waves penetrate the target of the magick, gently pervading it at reoccurring harmonic intervals, causing it to change through a constant immersion within subtle but powerfully radiating emanations.

The vortex is both a container of magickal effects as well as a mechanism to target and alter physical reality. The vortex can be simple or complex in its structure, since by its nature it contains all that is generated within it, having assimilated and emulated them perfectly within the place of their union. A vortex can even contain a cone or pyramid of power, where through mutual stimulation and climax, both mechanisms of empowerment achieve the highest level possible.

Power Octagon (Masculine & Feminine Conjoined)

The power octagon is a ritual structure of empowerment that uses both the spiral vortex and the pyramid of power together. The eight points of the magick circle, which include the four quarters and the four angles or cross-quarters, are used in two separate formulations to define the feminine and masculine expressions of power, one within the other. These two polarized powers are joined in the center of the circle, where the vortex core in the nadir is fused with the phallic pylon in the zenith. The center or core of this fused power is the mid-point between them both, where

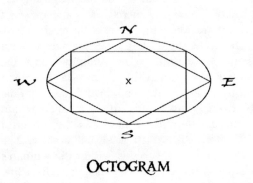

OCTOGRAM

stands the operator, connected to all eleven points simultaneously. The power octagon is used in the formulation of the magickal Elemental, and also forms the basis for other more complex ritual structures, which include the works of talismanic magick, theurgy and archeomancy.

Magickal Words of Power

Magickal words of power, chanting words or mantras and intoning magickal formulas are another form of raising magickal energy and empowering oneself. As any music lover can attest, sound is a vehicle that can produce resonance and impact the emotions directly. Mysterious words of power (verba ignota) have been a staple of magickal rites since the earliest times, and were a primary feature of the Greco-Egyptian magickal papyri. This tradition of using strange words of power is also found in numerous other magickal systems, most notably the Enochian system of magick, which uses the Enochian language in its invocations.

However, the words themselves have no real power other than what tradition and reputation has given them, and it is the imagination of the magician (awed by the archaic qualities of the words), and the methodology of intoning and voice projection, as well as the intention, that gives the arcane incantations their power.

Mantras and magickal formulas are a different case than words of power, and they typically have a very special meaning. They are usually used in the form of acronyms that have an imbedded significance known to the operator. Some have a traditional history of use, such as AGLA or I.N.R.I., others may be created by the magician for a specific need, such as drawing all the threads of a ritual together into a unified verbal expression. Mantras and magickal formulas are expressed in a repetitive and cyclic manner, using resonance and frequency to make them intensely impactful. Continually repeating or chanting a phrase or affirmation with great force can have quite a potent effect on one's psyche, making it a powerful realization.

Words of power or mantras require an effortless pronunciation and potent expression so that they flow when pronounced, and their expression is emotionally expressive, resonant and powerful. A magician learns to be a good word-smith, as well as a powerful speaker, developing a kind of actor's voice used to emphasize ritual verbiage.

Incantations are written up or memorized commands and exhortations that are poetically formulated, so that the phrases seem to come out as a kind of verbal music, whether rhyme or rhapsody is used. Incantations are used to summon or command forces or spirits, but it is done as a high form of verbal art.

49

All this, of course, would require a great deal of practice, so magicians do not use such techniques in their rituals without extensive rehearsals, at least until it is able to be executed flawlessly. Nothing could be more anticlimactic or ridiculous than someone stumbling through words of power at a critical point of a ritual.

Godhead Assumption

Assuming the Godhead is another method of magickal empowerment, and probably one of the most difficult, since it requires a deep level of possession trance as well as an affinity of the operator with the specific deity. In some systems of magick, such as the one presented in this book, Godhead assumption is a required state for the practice of ritual, in other systems, one either is deeply devoted to a godhead or it is omitted altogether. Those who omit the assumption or devotion to a deity are interested in the application of magick without any intruding spiritual dimension. However, based on the definition of magick, even such an arrogant perspective is changed and transformed over time.

Those who perform magick are engaged intimately with their higher self through the media of the super conscious mind. Nothing can dull or deflect the affects that this contact will have on an individual over time.

However, Godhead assumption requires a high degree of devotion and alignment to one's chosen Deity, as well as a highly practiced and accomplished technique of trance induction, which allows the Deity to superimpose itself upon the personality of the magician. Working magick while in this state of consciousness not only greatly empowers the magician, but it also makes the magick performed reach the highest levels of consciousness possible, making it the most effective kind of magick. Assumption of the Godhead as it is used in ritual magick was first proposed by Aleister Crowley, however, it is used in many African and Carribean religious traditions, and has its origins in Shamanism. It is the primary method whereby the religious adherent has an intimate encounter with his/her Deity, and is a hallmark of the Immanent Spirituality associated with earth based spiritual traditions.

Ecstatic Dance

Another method of empowerment is ecstatic dance or iterative ritual movement that has resonance and intensity. Dance can be used to promote a trance like state as well as generate magickal power and project it to its desired target. Ritual dance consists of repeated movements, usually in a circular motion, either deosil or widdershins, either around the periphery of the magick circle or within its boundaries.

The kind of movements that a magician can employ can be as simple as walking with purpose around the magick circle or turning in place or orbiting the magick circle like the whirling Dervish dance. The movements can be complex and even choreographed, using a variation of samba, bhangra, ragga, or even contact improvisation. Complex dancing usually involves more than one individual, while the simple routines are usually used by a single operator working alone.

Magickal dance has a pulse and a rhythm, and this is usually iterative, along with the accompanying body movements. But the pulse and movements follow a pattern of increased frequency that leads to a climactic crescendo, where the power is drawn up and projected outward to its intended target.

Breath Control

An intrinsic method of magickal empowerment, and one that is used in several of the methods mentioned above is breath control. The various techniques of breath control can be used alone to establish the proper mind state and even generate the required magickal energy and cause it to be projected outward.

Breath control, such as the four-fold breath, mantra and yantra yoga are used to produced the basic altered states of consciousness necessary for ritual magick. Other methods, such as bellows breath, cool breathing and hyperventilation (Lotus 7-breath) can be used to intensify one's awareness or even project the energy outwards and inwards.

Breath control is used to facilitate trance states, perform simple and complex bodily movements, and circulate the magickal energies through the body to promote healing and regeneration. Breath control is a known key to controlling conscious states. A magician spends a great deal of time learning to master these various techniques until they are automatic and intrinsic to magickal operations.

Use of Substances

One of the oldest methods of self empowerment, and perhaps one of the most abused, is the use of substances to alter consciousness; to imbue one's perceptions with greater subtlety and enhance the ability to sense and manipulate magickal power.

Herbal drugs have been a part of magickal practices since earliest times, and were a staple of the repertoire of the Shaman. Also included in this category are various devices, tools and fetishes. This would include such practices as bondage and discipline, the use of scourging, binding, and the mechanism of deliberately induced pain to generate power and even ecstasy. The magician can also use power objects, magickal tools, amulets and talismans, sigils and other magickal artifices to perform magickal operations and manipulate magickal power.

All of these methods are quite powerful when properly used in a disciplined manner, and all of them have also been abused by the ignorant and the jaded dilettante. Some of these methods will be covered in this book, others are treated in other sources. This category of tools and techniques is almost endless, since it is subject to the creative imagination and experimentation of the magician.

Sex Magick

The final method to be dealt with in this section is sex magick. There is no other mechanism of self empowerment and generating magickal energy that is more confused and abused than this one. The number of attested masters of sex magick seems limitless, and everyone has either an opinion or some experience with these techniques.

On the most essential level, sex magick is performed where the two celebrants have assumed their divinity through the assumption of the Godhead, and in this exalted state of consciousness, perform a series of steps that lead to the ultimate sacral consummation, the joining of the God and Goddess as an enactment of spiritual union.

A great deal of care and preparation goes into this act, so it is not the mere excuse for ritualized promiscuity. One could say that the practitioners of sex magick should be accomplished at both magick and at ritual sexuality before attempting to perform sex magick. A variety of other sacraments are used, as well as various tools, vestments, and fetishes to enhance and intensify the sexual activity. However, the principle concept behind sex magick is that it is performed in sacred space, where the celebrants have embodied the gods and assumed a state of consciousness far beyond that of the mundane world, and where the resultant orgasms are used to both empower and project that ecstatic energy to its intended target(s).

Suffice it to say, this method of empowerment and generating magickal power is probably the most difficult to achieve, and the easiest to fail at, for the obvious reason that the partner pair must act as one, and achieve their ecstasy at approximately the same time. The discipline of this system of magick consists of mutual orgasm within sacred space while undergoing a highly sacralized mind state, and it is a daunting discipline indeed.

3.3 Sacred Elements: Power Internalized

Aside from the ritual methods discussed above, there are direct ways of harnessing magickal power. These techniques, although ancient in source, are still practiced today and utilize several sacramental substances to achieve the realization of power.

A matrix has been constructed to divide these techniques into four basic categories: drugs (Water), dance and sex (Earth), meditation (Fire) and trance (Air).

Each category corresponds to one of the four elements, and in this way the four categories are qualified by associations with the elements.

* Drugs affect the mind and emotions (the domain of Water) causing dissociation and sometimes even hallucinations. They loosen our frame of reference (the quality of dissolving), which allows us to bend the laws of perception (refraction), and they assist us in the process of realizing the symbolic reality wherein all is one.

53

* Dance and sex affect the body and the emotions (the domain of Earth). Through experiencing the rhythmic cycles, we find ecstatic release and exhilaration.
* Meditation affects the mind and its processes of thinking (the domain of Fire), assisting us in control of our thoughts and impulses, and to analyze the source of our needs and drives.
* Trance is the assumption of an obsession that joins together and locks the dual processes of will and feeling (the domain of Air). Trance states assist the magician to be highly focused to the degree of extreme concentration. This allows for the magician to be able to concentrate exclusively on a single thing without interruption or distraction.

Each of these categories has within it four specific possibilities, one for each of the four Elements, thus revealing a total of 16 specific techniques. Whereas the categories are quite general, each of the techniques within each category is more specific. All cause the transformation of consciousness with distinctly different effects.

Each seeks to methodologically control some aspect of the senses. Over stimulating the senses is attained by an exterior effect as in dance and trance or by an inner effect such as drugs and meditation, or the use of sacraments aiding the magician's quest for empowerment. This type of mind alteration illustrates the passive and active modes of the senses as they are being transformed. The assumption of the sacramental power of the Element is done while focusing the mind on symbols of transformation, so the resultant alteration in consciousness produces profound transformations in the magician.

Table of the Sixteen Sacramental Elements

Base/Qualifier	Fire	Water	Air	Earth
Fire	Mental Meditation	Meditation upon the void	Breath Control	Physical Discipline
Water	Hallucinatory substances or caffeine	Liquid spirits	Aromatic substances	Herbal roots, royal jelly, chocolate
Air	Guided visualized trance	Skrying/Astral Projection	Power trance - intense focus	Body trance - shape changing
Earth	Fascination	Massage - healing	Karezza - bondage/discipline	Dance - sex magick

Fire

Since meditation is the category representing the Element of Fire, there are four techniques of meditation that would represent this element as it is qualified by one of the other three elements and by itself.

Fire of Fire

Fire of Fire would represent a meditation technique that wholly embraces the intellect. Therefore, the Eastern tradition's technique of Vedanta Yoga, which succeeds in intellectually grasping the concept of Deity through the process of negation (i.e., the neti-neti Atman method, "God is not this, not that"), would be an appropriate example.

Water of Fire

Water of Fire would denote a system of meditation that focuses upon the void of consciousness, and so it would be analogous to the techniques of zazen (the technique of gradual mind reduction until nothing is left but non-dual being) as practiced in Zen meditation.

Air of Fire

Air of Fire would represent various techniques of breath control or Pranayama yoga.

Earth of Fire

Earth of Fire emphasizes the mind controlling the body, thus exemplifying some form of Hatha Yoga or the martial arts.

Water

The Element of Water is represented by various techniques of substance or drug usage.

Fire of Water

Fire of Water would represent the most potent mind-altering substance known to humanity, LSD It is worth noting that the ancients possessed this drug through the occurrence of argot of rye, and they supposedly collected and used it in the potion served at the Eleusinian Mysteries. A suitable alternative would be strong Turkish coffee, or the mixture of red ginseng and royal jelly.

Water of Water

Water of Water is represented by the most common drug known to humanity, alcohol. This sacrament is usually consumed as wine or beer, but can also be taken in its distilled form as brandy, whisky or vodka. (A preeminent form of this sacrament would be Absinthe.) The Water of Water can also be represented by various derivatives of opium.

Air of Water

Air of Water is represented by either cannabis sativa, cannabis indica (hashish), methyl amphetamines or by very strong tobaccos, as that found in expensive cigars.

Earth of Water

Earth of Water is represented by potent herbal drugs such as psilocybin mushrooms, cocaine, ayahuasca, peyote, aminitas muscaria mushrooms, deadly nightshade and datura. A suitable alternative for Earth would be sufficient quantities of baker's chocolate or pure honey (royal jelly).

A Note On The Use of Drugs

The practicing magician is cautioned with regards to use of substances, especially those that are illegal or potentially harmful. Although controlled substances were used by magicians in the past to assist in the acquisition of powers and transcendental mind-states, and are still used by native populations throughout the world, use of controlled substances is illegal in many countries in the West. The matrix of sacraments includes legal substitutes so that the magician has a choice of using legal rather than illegal substances. The magician may also choose to ignore the use of any substances at all. The above items are intended for informational purposes only and are not to be misconstrued as an invitation for their use.

The author neither condemns nor condones the use of controlled substances. The student who chooses to use them is advised to be familiar with them, including their effects and associated toxicity. Their use should also be in a controlled setting and monitored by someone who is not partaking. Some drugs are poisonous and the level of dosage should be carefully researched before ingesting to avoid harmful effects.

The important concept here is that drugs and potions are an aid for the magician to adopt the proper mind-state for a ritual working. They are a means and not an end. The magician must also be aware of the legal implications of using controlled substances as well as the social stigma. However, the practice of magick is an ancient discipline and cannot be affected by the duplicity and insincerity of a society that is addicted to sugar, alcohol, caffeine, tobacco, chocolate and various pharmaceuticals, but who prohibits the use of marijuana, LSD, peyote, ayahuasca and psilocybin in controlled settings.

Air

The Element of Air is symbolized by various techniques of trance.

Fire of Air

Fire of Air would signify techniques of visualization or a method of guided visualized trance induction.

Water of Air

Water of Air would correspond to the technique of astral projection or dream programming.

Air of Air

Air of Air would represent what is called the power-trance, being a potent form of focusing that resembles a type of intensive self-willed mental concentration.

Earth of Air

Earth of Air would symbolize the trance technique of shape-changing, wherein the operator projects the trance state through the physical body to emulate a totem animal. This state also assists one in the phenomenon of fire walking and in being physically pierced by sharp objects without experiencing any harm.

Earth

The Element of Earth is associated with variations of dance and sexuality. It is easy for anyone to see how these two concepts are linked and related to Earth.

Fire of Earth

Fire of Earth would embody the technique of fascination or enchantment that is an empowerment experienced by the enhanced visual effect of one's image (i.e., seeing one's self in a mirror as handsome or beautiful). The eyes are the means for inducing as well as receiving this effect. Fascination is a two-way form of visual empowerment because it affects the one projecting his/her image as well as the one who's receiving it. It's also called *casting a glamour*, but it can be used like skrying (crystal gazing) where the unconscious mind is projected into one's visual perception.

Water of Earth

Water of Earth would be symbolized by various techniques of body massage and physical healing by the laying on of hands.

Air of Earth

Air of Earth would be characterized by the technique of Karezza, as used in sex magick, where the male withholds the ejaculation of semen during orgasm. Also the methods of bondage and discipline would apply to Air of Earth, as well as abstinence from all sexuality.

Earth of Earth

Earth of Earth would signify the techniques of ecstatic dance (similar to the Samba, a modern derivation of primitive devotional dancing) and ultimately, the dance of life itself, sexual intercourse.

The hidden sacraments of the Earth Element also consist in the various bodily fluids associated with life and ecstatic union (fresh blood, spittle, semen, menses, urine, feces, etc.). These have been used by magicians as agents of power since the dawn of humanity, though they do not necessarily need to be used today.

3.4 The Four Levels of Magickal Power

The four levels of magickal power characterize methods of perceiving or projecting magickal energy. This topic has been covered fairly extensively in *Disciple's Guide*, but we will briefly review some points in order to expound further.

Since all magickal power is symbolized by the joining of the archetypal masculine and feminine, then the *first level of charging and empowerment occurs with the joining of a male and female celebrant*. Whether that joining results in actual coitus or is done in symbolic token does not lessen the impact of the ritual action.

The *second level of magickal power is the creation and generation of magickal sacraments, and their application as a mechanism for making objects sacred and fostering an alignment between individuals and their Deities*. A magickal sacrament is made when an ordinary substance is imbued and empowered by a celebrant acting as an agent for the Deity.

Sacraments include the lustral or holy water (salt and water), wine or ale, cakes or bread, and oils or lotions. There are many variations on these four basic sacraments, but the four consist of the sacraments of aspurgation (sprinkling holy water), communion (serving sacramental food and drink), and chrismation (applying sacral oil, anointing).

The *third level of magickal power is the abstract production of magickal devices, whether drawn in the air with wand or dagger, or as talismans, amulets and magickal illustrations.* Visualizations and ritual movements can also be considered under this level of magickal power.

The *fourth level of magickal power is the methods of transference and association.* Tools, objects and anything else that is used in conjunction with the workings of ritual magick gain by association, a magickal power all of their own. The fourth level of magickal power is also found at various locations or power spots, and these can have a traditional association with some historical or legendary magickal environment, or it can be purely in the mind of the magician, where a mythical place is superimposed upon a mundane location, transforming it into a domain of magick and wonder.

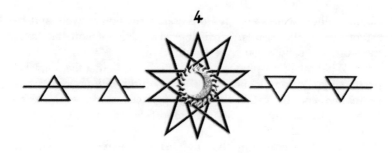

The Magickal Identity

4.1 The Magickal Personality

When choosing to work magickal rituals and establish a magickal dimension in life, the necessity arises to develop an identity distinct from mundane roles and responsibilities.

While it has always been the practice of magicians to wear robes and elaborate costumes for the theatrical presentation of magickal ritual, exotic garb has never been merely a matter of exterior adornment. When attired, the magician becomes a different person – a magickal being. The robes, makeup, masks, jewelry, perfumes and various props represent an inner transformation of consciousness that profoundly alters one's sense of identity.

In the altered field of magickal consciousness, the symbol of an item becomes that which it represents. For instance, a man may believe that the spirit of Merlin is strongly connected to him, therefore, he would consider himself a spiritual son of this historical and mythical personage, and may rightfully claim all the powers and prerogatives of the great Merlin.

This connection could never be proven, and would probably be considered dubious or even silly by someone outside this personal magickal process. However, to the magician, this belief would be part of his individual magickal mythology and would assist him in the working of magickal rituals in the guise of Merlin. Therefore, he may dress and be made up to look like Merlin the Magician, play acting the part of that venerable sage.

The power of association would make it true, so that through this process, he would actually become a realized personification of

Merlin. Others would perceive this transformation as well, and be astonished at the results, consisting as it does of both an inner transformation and an outer personification.

What many neophytes may fail to realize is that the magickal personality is carefully chosen and built up through various trance techniques and the establishment of personal mythology. So the garb and make up are not as important as the actual inner corresponding change.

A magician carefully chooses a magickal name and a motto or slogan that identifies spiritual ambitions to formulate an integrated magickal personality with a personal mythology and associated beliefs. The intention of the magickal personality consists of the aspirations and desires of the magician, which should be ennobling and represent a principal part of the process of the magician's spiritual growth. The importance of a magickal identity is that it directs the awareness of the self into the realms of the spirit, where it gains great personal meaning and significance.

To the magician, the cult of the magickal personality ultimately establishes a sense of history and meaningful evolution, a strong sense of personal identity and a potent sense of purpose and direction. Thus the power inherent in the magickal personality is that it resolves the three most important issues of human existence: the definition of self (identity), the establishment of personal history and the determination of personal destiny. These can be summed up in the three questions that the existential individual seeks to find answers for: "Who am I?", "Where have I been and why?" and "What is my goal, my purpose?"

4.2 The Magickal Name and Motto

The selection of a magickal name is an important and significant task. The taking of a magickal name is the first step to dedicating the self to the practice of magick. The name assumes an identity associated exclusively with magick, and like the tools and equipment dedicated to the work of ritual, the magickal personality derived from that name becomes itself a magickal tool, assisting in the transformation of the mundane into the spiritual. And like the magickal tools, the magickal name becomes a reality within the mind-state associated with magick.

Name & Imago

When choosing a name, the magician usually selects one associated with magickal or mythical beings such as gods or goddesses, historical persons, meaningful concepts or even places or objects of a magickal quality. The name can be simple, such as Merlin, or complex and contrived, such as Stella Solaria Amadeae (Sun-Star, Beloved of the Goddess).

The name is also associated with a personality (persona), represented by attitudes, beliefs and a personal image. The name simply unites all the components of the persona into an integrated whole, a veritable dynamic personality called the *imago* by magicians.

As a form of practice to invoke the magician's imago, the dressing and adornment of the magician is followed by an intense self-scrutiny in a full-length mirror, with the eyes of the magician and that of the reflection locked into a fixed gaze that becomes the basis of a fascination trance. The magician then chants the magickal name repeatedly, along with other descriptive qualifiers that reinforce the overall effect of the magickal personality. This technique will complete the process of assuming a magickal identity that makes it fully believable and a seamless extension of one's normal personality.

It is also important to note that the chief technique used in developing the magickal personality is known as self-worship or self-love, hence the above technique of fascination. This may seem rather narcissistic, but because of its spiritual intention, it is actually the positive celebration of the connection between the mundane self and the Deity. The magician is actually taking delight in bathing, anointing and vesting for the purpose of furthering the love and appreciation for the chosen Deity. Thus the magician acts as if he or she were a suitor for the personal love and affection of this Deity; a very noble and selfless operation. But the self is not denied, it is rather transformed and made eminently worthy of respect and love by the Deity. The adornment is merely an outward reflection of the love and esteem the magician has for the Deity.

To give the Deity that which one does not highly regard is to cheapen and even degrade the offering. The self is the ultimate offering to the Deity, and it is only a fitting one when that self is loved, cherished and beautifully adorned. In this fashion of self-love, the magician approaches the Deity, armed with

63

self-esteem and personal empowerment, thus being capable of assuming the powers, authority and prerogatives of the Deity. This is the personal state of mind that must be established before any ritual magick is performed if that working is to be guaranteed a successful outcome. The operator must become a God/dess within the context of the ritual and in the confines of the temple or grove; for in no other guise can the archetypal and abstract symbols of being be manipulated.

Motto

The magickal motto represents a kind of saying or quote that fully captures the intention of the magician. The motto can be written in one's native tongue (a living language) or constructed in some exotic foreign language, preferably one associated with magick and mystery such as the languages of Latin, Classical Greek, Classical Hebrew, Classical Arabic, Aramaic, ancient Egyptian, Old Gaelic, Sanskrit or some other dead language.

The use of a dead language gives the mind a sense of antiquity that acts as a magnet for the psychic images of ancient times, lost worlds and their historical and mythical associations. Also it would seem that magicians love dead languages because they are procurers of the obscure, and they look for any excuse to transform something common into something unusual.

Dedication

Along with the magickal name and motto is another facet of the magickal personality that is very important for the effective working of ritual magick - the dedication.

The magickal name and motto imply a certain dedication and alignment with the spiritual process of ritual magick. However, the explicit statement of one's goals, desires, aspirations and one's spiritual alignment is a profound and necessary step to completing the magickal personality. This explicit statement is known as the Dedication to the Art of Magick and represents the accumulation of personal magickal beliefs that ultimately fuse together to form the magician's *Egregore* (group-mind or body of light); this is a spiritual dimension to the self that is both integral and central to the spiritual development of the magician.

The declaration of the magickal dedication becomes a powerful statement of spiritual alignment, and it's the ultimate mechanism through which the Higher Self or Holy Guardian Angel is finally able to manifest. The magickal dedication is the channel through which the Absolute Spirit communicates to the magician, and it is a bond that allows the magician to temporarily assume the powers and prerogatives of the incarnate God without committing a blasphemy or erroneous presumption.

The dedication first begins as a simple goal, which is little more than the desire to master the art of magick, and develops over time to a complete identification with all matters of magick and the occult (the consuming desire "to know everything"). It ultimately establishes for the magician a role in the continually evolving process of the spiritual evolution of all humanity. At a particular point along this continuum, the magician feels the need to make a personal dedication to the process of magick and to the service of a specific Deity.

The magickal dedication is a requirement for the successful undertaking of all higher forms of ritual magick. Magicians realize the need to state unequivocally their intentions regarding the use of magick and to whom they are answerable for its use. This causes a certain resonance to occur within their spiritual being, thus making them a responsible vehicle for the greater spiritual process to manifest. Magicians are Priests/Priestesses and a divine channel of transformation, and the alignment to a specific Deity is an obligatory step prior to the assumption of its qualities and powers.

The taking of a magickal name and motto and the assumption of a magickal personality must occur before the alignment of the magician to their personal Deity, and yet it also prepares the way for this occurrence. The fully developed magickal personality ultimately leads the magician to the source of its power, which is the emanation of a personal god or goddess. So the dedication becomes the final link that leads one from the mundane and physical to the spiritual world, through the spiritual gateway forged by the artifice of ritual magick. However, magicians are aware of the fact that they act as an agent of the Deity and cannot perform the art of ritual magick alone unless they act unethically. Without the sponsorship of the Deity, magick becomes a common psychic occurrence, or worse yet, the petty and egotistic acquisition of personal power, or even complete self-delusion.

In a ritual setting, when a magician verbally declares a carefully composed dedication speech, it has a powerful effect. The result causes the magician to act in such a way so that magick becomes a unifying principle in his or her life. Thus, for the practitioner magick becomes an end unto itself. The magician seeks to ultimately become one with the Deity, to be completely subsumed within its Being, and act as a perfect and unbiased channel for the manifestation of its divine destiny.

This dedication is declared during an initiation ritual, within a consecrated and charged temple or grove. It becomes, for a time, the sole spiritual purpose of the magician.

It's assumed that this dedication is not fixed, but constantly evolving along with the knowledge and experience of the magician.

The magician states a spiritual affirmation in front of witnesses, after having been purified, charged and properly aligned to the chosen Deity. The dedication should always begin with the desire to know so that the magician will learn and grow. The desire for knowledge gives birth to the desire for self-perfection, ultimately leading to serving and assisting the world in its path to perfection. The dedication begins the magician's spiritual process of unfolding, and subsequent dedications hasten that process and further refine it. In this manner, the powers of continuous self-transformation are unleashed and the never-ending process of transformation is begun.

The aforementioned considerations all form the preparatory tasks that are enacted prior to the circle consecration ritual. The magician must be fully prepared to work magick before the working space is purified and charged. Without the correct mind-state, a ritual becomes meaningless and ineffective, a series of actions without any purpose.

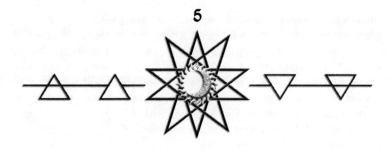

Techniques of Mind Control

The core discipline in the practice of ritual magick is control of the mind. Learning to master magick requires an ability to master the mind, control one's focus of attention, attune oneself to deep internal sensitivities, and to assume higher states of consciousness. Mental control is also the key to the manipulation of energies and symbols of transformation, which produce the phenomena of magick. Mind control assists the magician in experiencing the highest strata of consciousness that occupies the domain of Spirit.

In the *Disciple's Guide to Ritual Magick*, the topics of occult psychology and basic mind control have already been extensively covered. Therefore I will only recap these topics so I may elaborate on more advanced techniques.

5.1 Introduction

Deliberate variation and control of the breath is the primary mechanism for mental control. This may seem like a very unusual connection to make, yet it is accepted as a great truth among the practitioners of Yoga and other meditative systems of the East.

To these practitioners, the art of meditation and contemplation is often referred to as "the science of breath". However, the more mundane truth represents a few simple rules of physiology; a deliberate and focused alternation of breathing changes the focus of the mind and decouples it from its normal preoccupations. An increase in the frequency of breathing causes more oxygen to be circulated through the brain, which in turn changes the mode of consciousness that one is experiencing. Taken to extremes, such as in hyperventilation, accelerated breathing can even cause vertigo and unconsciousness. However, practiced in moderation, breath control can modify consciousness so as to increase one's focus or dissolve it altogether in trance. The artful combination of redirecting conscious focus and either increasing or decreasing oxygen flow to the brain causes an array of alternate states of consciousness to be readily available to the practicing mystic and magician. This is important because the mind in its normal state is neither sensitive nor focused enough to recognize the effects of subtle spiritual phenomena and the higher states of consciousness that embody them.

To perform magickal rituals requires the ability to see and experience conscious reality in a completely different manner, so one can perceive what the mind normally senses as incomprehensible and inexplicable. Therefore, we need to examine the techniques of mind control so as to ensure that we have the mechanisms in place to alter consciousness.

Mind control is an art form since there are many ways that one can practice it. It is up to each individual to find their own unique combination of practices and employ them in a successful manner. Mind control is also a science since specific practices consistently produce certain mind-states. This is something that can be easily shown as an objective fact by all practitioners.

Mind control uses four practical disciplines to alter consciousness, and these are asana, pranayama, mantra, and mandala.

Asana

Asana is the bodily posture that one adopts to perform the exercises of mind control. The asana must be comfortable but not so comfortable that it allows one to fall asleep. It must allow the practitioner to maintain an effortless posture while focusing on other areas of body and the mind. A body that is uncomfortable and not relaxed cannot begin to assume the proper mental state to perform these exercises. It can be a simple static posture or it can be a ritualized form of moving exercises, like the Sun Salutation in Hatha Yoga. It can even be a form of repetitive dance, such as the movements that Sufi dancers make while performing a zikr. A dynamic asana can even encompass an entire ritual.

The body is the place where magick begins and ends. The mystic and magician learn to integrate the body and mind into a seamless whole - known as the body-mind in Yoga. The asana is principally understood as the seating posture used for meditation, a relaxed state or position of repose, where one may effortlessly engage in self-scanning, or focusing on specific aspects of breathing and bodily awareness. The asana in yoga begins with the seating posture of the half or full lotus, and climaxes in the head stand and Sun Salutation. The asana can also capture movement, and ultimately, becomes the vehicle for the performance of ritualized actions in sacred space.

Prana

Prana is breath, and breath control is called pranayama (literally breath restriction or control). Breath control acts as the basic set of exercises used to control consciousness. It can vary in extremes from the most restive and relaxing continuous breathing, to the most intense forms of hyperventilation.

The simplest method of breath control is simply to count the breaths as they occur when one is breathing in a relaxed repose. The basic method is the four-fold breath.

The next method begins to use some of the many methods of prana-yama, and is known as cool breathing. It is the focused breathing through pursed lips of both inhalation and exhalation. The lips are formed as one would say the letter "U", and one breathes through this narrow aperture. Cool breathing is used to direct and intensify one's conscious focus, and is used to draw attention to a specific ritual event as it is happening.

Hyperventilation, or the Lotus 7-breath, is used to promote a brief and powerful ecstatic trance; to send one completely out of the body into the spirit world. The magician uses cool breathing and breath counting throughout the performance of ritual to establish, alter and maintain the proper mind state. The Lotus 7-breath (accelerating breathing) has a very specific use, and is seldom used more than once in an entire ritual, if used at all.

Mantra and Mandala

Mantra and mandala (yantra) techniques control the senses of hearing and seeing and restrict them to a single focused sensorial input. This causes that sensorial input to become overloaded. The practice of mantra is where the practitioner intones a word or phrase over and over again, allowing the sound to resonate deep into the vocal cords and nasal passages. The single word or phrase completely captivates the focus of the mind, and all else is ignored as irrelevant.

From the basic mind state as established by breath counting, the magician will employ words and phrases, intoning and repeating them in a seemingly endless cycle, ensuring that the mind focuses on nothing else but the perfect intonation and recitation of the mantra. If the word or phrase has a powerful significance to the magician, then the mantra will have more effect when intoned repeatedly. However, significant words that have no real meaning, but are imbued with tradition are also allowed, such as the ubiquitous Aum. The practice of mantra yoga can easily lead to the magickal intoning of incantations and word-based spells, creating a powerful association between special words of power and their effect on the mind and soul. A mantra is used in conjunction with breath control to produce the various states of trance that are necessary for the immersion of the self within transcendental states of consciousness.

The practice of mandala involves the practitioner staring fixedly at a complex linear diagram or meaningful symbolic image. The mandalic image (mandala or yantra) is an image constructed with known visual ambiguities that produce the illusion of movement or visual transformation. Staring fixedly at such an image or diagram, and negating all other visual stimuli or thoughts, will cause visual distortions and even complete hallucinations.

Visual control and directed visualization are very important tools in the repertoire of the mystic and the magician. A yantra is an ambiguous geometric diagram that causes visual distortions when normally viewed, and even stronger effects when stared at. Modern western versions of a yantra can be found in the etchings of M. C. Escher, where visual paradoxes are graphically represented in an ingenious and artistic manner, confounding the eye and the mind.

The occultist uses similar diagrams to represent the spiritual cosmos, and these, such as the Tree of Life for instance, can produce powerful visual effects when stared at in a fixed manner. Like the mantra, a yantra or occult diagram should have a deep and meaningful significance to the operator, so its effect will be more potent to the mind. Certain rules in the form of yantra should also be used, such as the use of vibrating or contrasting colors, concentric lines or shapes, and fractal structures representing the recursive quality of the mind itself. A mandala, like a mantra, has a magickal use in the methods of directed or guided visualization, and the combination of incantation and directed visualization in ritual produce the sensory perceptions of magick: the mundane world overlaid by the world of Spirit.

These two practices, mantra and mandala, when combined with breath control, can produce very deep states of mental absorption or abstraction, accompanied with a hypnotic trance. This trance-like state can be mild or it can be very deep, depending on the intensity of the exercise, and the practitioner can use a combination of techniques to more deeply and profoundly affect the mind. Mind control techniques are used to produce various levels of absorption and hypnotic trance, and these levels of trance are the basic states of consciousness that are used to perform ritual magick and to channel the Deity.

Trance

Trance is not the final destination for the practicing magician; it is in fact the beginning or fundamental state of consciousness used to perform ritual magick. Three practices are performed by the magician while in this trance state, and these are meditation or contemplation, ritual magickal performance (liturgies) and spiritual alignment or the assumption of Deity. All three of these practices have a single operation that is performed, and that is the immersion of the mind in spiritual sentiments, symbols, liturgies and devotions while in a trance state. This combination of trance state and spiritual symbols (symbols of transformation) causes a powerful transformation of consciousness, and allows for the manifestation of higher states of consciousness associated with the spiritual dimension and the higher self. The practices of contemplation and spiritual alignment are embraced solely by the mystic, whereas the magician also practices borrowed liturgies as ritual magickal operations and the exercises of the personal assumption of Deity.

Contemplation occurs when the mystic or magician concentrates exclusively on deep spiritual topics and mystical paradoxes. In contemplation, the magician uses the methodology of monitoring thoughts and re-focusing the mind when it strays in order to form a continuous detached awareness of the topic and one's reaction and sentiments to it.

Alignment is found in the exoteric spiritual devotions that one adopts to promote a close intimacy with the Deity. Ritual magick consists of the various rites and liturgies that are used to raise consciousness as energy, and to project it both within and without the self, causing various profound mental manifestations to occur to one's spirit, soul, mind, body and the world at large. Assumption consists of the specific practices that cause the magician to briefly attain conscious union with the Deity, so that the two personalities are blended transcendentally into one.

The four methods of posture, breath, mantra and mandala mentioned above are used together harmoniously to build the proper mind state conducive to the real work of the mystic and the magician, which is contemplation, meditation and ritual performance. The mystic focuses more on meditation and contemplation, and the magician focuses more on ritual performance. However, simply stated, these three techniques of expanding the basic meditative mind-state use the powerful effect of symbols of transformation to induce deep conscious transformations.

All of these transformative symbols, in their various forms, are embedded in the religions of the world, both past and the present, and only require one to think upon them in a focused and disciplined manner to produce a spiritual effect. However, if they are focused upon while in an altered state of consciousness produced by the techniques of asana, breath control, mantra and mandala, they will produce a potent conscious transformation.

To practice the art of contemplation, students focus on a symbol of transformation and allow no other thoughts to intervene. They may impassively observe all of the mental associations that such a focused mental concentration produces, but do not allow them to distract from the single objective of that focus.

Similar to mantra and mandala, contemplation causes one's perception to become profoundly altered, and opens a gateway in the mind to areas that transcend the self in time and space. One may assume a simple asana to achieve this transcendental transformation, or one may also engage movement, and perform symbolic ritual actions within the context of liturgical or devotional rites, or magickal rites.

The meditation practices employed by the mystic and the magician start out at the same place, but the magician engages in additional practices to channel the Deity and its transforming powers into the mundane world. This causes a furthering of ambitions or divine plan of that Deity.

Ritual magicians cultivate powerful transcendental states of consciousness that facilitate trance and the performance of ritual; they all work within the same exalted mental state, which is to be immersed in the Spiritual Domain. This state of affairs occurs whether the magician is aware of it or not, and it ultimately causes an awareness of the self as Spirit, or as the God/dess Within. The system of magick that is promoted in this work uses the assumption of the Godhead directly, and all else occurs within the manifestation of that transformative dimension.

The five methods of posture, breath, mantra, mandala and trance represent the corner stone of practices and disciplines for the active magician. They must be ultimately mastered either as the essential tools of the mystic seeking to be absorbed in Deity, or the magician who seeks to manifest the sacramental powers of that Deity into the physical world.

Intermediate magicians should master these techniques to the point where they are automatic. By extending them using more developed and deeper methodologies, the production of greater magickal affects and mystical realizations will occur.

5.2 Intermediate Techniques of Mind Control

The intermediate techniques that I wish to incorporate into this work come from the teachings and books written by Franz Bardon. I feel that it is important to know a little bit about him so as to understand the nature of his work and why I feel that it is so important, and a necessary part of this work. In appendix I, you will find biographical and historical information about Bardon in order to put the following text into greater context.

It is sufficient to say that Franz Bardon's influence on practical magickal and Hermetic traditions is quite profound, but only an elite few are intimately aware of these influences, and few outside of that group ever acknowledge him as their source.

Bardon's magickal philosophy is quite simple and elegant, and is found embedded in many other current magickal practices in the Western Mystery tradition.[7] Many of his concepts can be found in other unrelated traditions, even including one or two traditions of Wicca and Neopaganism. My own magickal techniques are suffused

---

7   See the online Wikipedia entry for Franz Bardon -
http://en.wikipedia.org/wiki/Franz_Bardon

with concepts derived from Bardon's writings, almost to the point where they are unrecognizable.

In his book, *Initiation into Hermetics*, Bardon declares that the highest principle is called Akasha[8], which contains the integral godhead and all archetypal forms, and it is the product of, and binds together the four Elements. The four Elements are both metaphysical concepts as well as actual physical phenomena. The magician uses a form of symbolic visualization to connect with, draw in, manipulate and project outwards, these four elements.

Bardon was the first magickal occult writer to postulate that the four elements were the building blocks of the four universes of the akashic mental, astral and physical planes. The four elements are found blending together in three of these worlds, representing the three levels of the elements as mental, astral and physical. The key to mastering the four elements is to know and recognize them as they exist in these three levels. The hermetic magician uses all three levels to aid his ability to manifest and manipulate the elements, and thereby empowers himself and his work with their magickal effect. The level of Akasha, though, represents the four elements in harmonic fusion (union), and it is the Akasha that is most responsible for the miraculous ability to perceive, align oneself, manipulate, and project the four elements for various magickal effects.

Comparing this definition of Akasha with my own term "World of Spirit", they seem to be identical in definition and function.

Initiation into Hermetics is a training system divided into ten practical steps. Each step is divided into three sub-steps, which includes training on the three bodies - mental, astral and physical. These are designed to incrementally develop the practicing magician in a balanced and effective manner, with exercises and practices for the mental, psychic and physical levels.

The first four steps are concerned with self-analysis, concentration, breathing, visualization, and the channeling or self-inducting, storing and projecting of the elements. Some ritual mnemonics and techniques are taught in the fourth chapter as well, but these seem to function as triggers for methodologies already practiced - a short hand method of gaining the results of an

---

8   See *Initiation into Hermetics* by Franz Bardon – p. 18 -21

intensive and time consuming technique. The techniques mastered in chapters two through four of the book are most relevant to this work, and we shall be covering a variation of them below. It is assumed that practicing magicians are already familiar with their own inner self and soul dimensions, so we don't have to revisit the methodologies covered in the first chapter, which is self analysis.

In order to accumulate, manipulate and project elemental magickal powers, magicians must learn to perceive them, induct them into their body, and then visually project them to a specific purpose, and also to drain the self of any leftover accumulated elemental energies. All of these procedures use forms of visualization, which is to say that they are not concerned with actual physical phenomena. They represent a method of projecting a visualized perception upon normal reality and so infusing it with a magickal perspective, which does produce a corresponding physical phenomenon in the body.

These practices are important because they give the magician an effective method of channeling magickal powers, which would be invisible and imperceptible to the normal conscious mind. So we will be gathering together specific exercises from steps two, three, and four of Bardon's book that are concerned with the accumulation of the elements, and the loading or projecting of that accumulated energy into objects or the temple room itself. These exercises are practiced and performed separately until they are mastered, but are ultimately used in the rituals that generate magickal powers, giving them a tangible and physical quality that they would not ordinarily possess.

5.2.2 Conscious Pore Breathing – Breathing With the Body

Step 2 of the Physical training is "pore breathing".[9] This technique is an extension of the magician's already mastered regimen of breathing exercises. It's important for you to engage in practices of bodily purification and being aware of how hot and cold ablutions open and close the pores of your skin, and the use of wash cloths and scrub brushes clear out and activate your pores in a healthful manner. As magicians, we are taught to become very attuned and sensitively aware to the pores of our skin, which puts into our mind

---

9   See *Initiation into Hermetics* by Franz Bardon – p. 71

the ability to sense phenomena occurring within them or through them. These preparations prepare us for the next step, which is learning to absorb or actively breathe through the pores of our skin.

As you perform the usual breathing exercises (4-fold breath), you begin to notice and sense the pores of the skin breathing in and out in the same manner as their lungs. An extension of this exercise is to breathe in certain sentiments, such as good health, well being, or perfect relaxation through the lungs and the pores of the skin, sensing these positive and life affirming qualities saturating yourself to the point of blissful satiety.

Likewise, you may also exhale out through your lungs and pores feelings that are negative or associated with disease, such as fear, restlessness, discomfort, and to some degree, even a certain amount of pain. This exercise should be performed so often that you can automatically perform it by simply thinking of making a self-adjustment, and then either breathing in or exhaling out as needed. This exercise should also be performed as part of the meditation session, particularly to settle your mind and body, and bring in a degree of self resolution and inner peace - an important basic mind-state to the practice of any kind of magick.

5.2.3 Acquiring and Projecting the Elements Through Pore Breathing

The next set of exercises[10], which deals with breathing and projecting the four elements, builds on the technique of pore breathing. It is essential that the elements enter the body and fill it up through the organ of the skin instead of just the lungs.

The purpose of breathing in, accumulating and projecting out the four elements is that it assists in raising and channeling magickal energy as well as the perception of it visually and physically.

The first exercise concerns itself with breathing in one of the four elements. You should sit in a comfortable asana and holding either string of beads or knots to act as a counter in your hands.

Then imagine yourself sitting in a world consisting of just that pure element, whether it is fire, water, air or earth. The quality

---

10   See *Initiation into Hermetics* by Franz Bardon – Step 3 Psychic Training p. 79 – 83, and Step 3 Physical Training, p. 83 - 87

of that element is noted and imagined to such a degree that the magician can almost physically experience it.

Perceive the elements as follows:
Fire - expansive, dynamic, brilliant and giving off an intense heat.
Water - fluidic, cold, passive, and luminescent.
Air - light, warm, volatile and scintillating.
Earth - cold, dense, heavy, inert, dark, but also containing an embedded vital force.

In addition, the four elements are also perceived as being energies that have a specific color, although these are more symbolic than actual *(fire being red, water, blue-green, air, azure, and earth, yellow, grey or black)*.

Imagine the element as concisely as possible, and then begin to perform the exercise of inhaling that element into the body through both the nose and the pores. You should perceive the element filling your body, and affecting it intensely with the qualities of that element.

For instance, if you are breathing in fire, then you should feel an intense heat condensing inside your body as more fire element is sucked within you. Use the string of beads or knots as a means of counting the inhalation breaths, and you should start performing this exercise with seven breaths, and steadily increase that amount until twenty or thirty breaths are achieved.

Correspondingly, also exhale the accumulated element out through both the lungs and the pores, using the same number of inhalation breaths, and empty the body of the accumulated element.

This is a control feature that teaches you to carefully use everything that enters your body and so avoid trapping energy in it, creating unwanted effects. This exercise is a kind of energy decompression that is quite important. You learn to accumulate an element in the body through pore breathing, and how to empty the body of the same element thus accumulated.

It is recommended that you breathe in and exhale out only through the nose, and not through the open mouth, perhaps to use the narrow aperture of the nostrils as a governor to control the amount of element absorbed or extracted. I have found that you may also use the open mouth, and inhale and exhale through the pursed aperture of the lips, like cool breathing.

This method is actually even more efficacious in controlling and concentrating the intake and extraction of an element, and it greatly intensifies the effect.

The next couple of exercises build on the ability to visualize the inhalation and exhalation of an element, by visualizing that element accumulating in a specific part of the body, and these are part of the psychic training in step four[11].

It's also recommended that you not accumulate energy in either the heart or the brain. For our purposes, we wish to accumulate the element energy in the hands, where it can be used to project that element into a substance or an object for further magickal use (a sigil or a sacrament). You can also exhale the element to fill up the room or temple where you are sitting, alternating with accumulating and loading that environment with the appropriate element.

These two techniques allow you to perceive and participate in the raising of energy in the temple or grove, as well as projecting the element through your hands into a tool, and then into an object or substance. They also assist in achieving a powerful visualization technique that gives a more potent physical and psychic quality to the magickal power that you raise and project in your magickal rituals. The more developed the visualization the more real it seems, and the more effective it will be in the physical world.

By using the techniques of channeling the elements, imprinting them with positive and life-affirming desires, the four elements are visualized. The visualizations are expanded, giving you a powerful tool to manipulate all aspects of your mental and physical world, and to draw in all good things needful and desired by yourself. These additional techniques, added to the ones already mastered, produce a formidable array of methods and practices to control the self, the mind and project magickal power into the world. These methodologies are integral to the practice of magick; effective rituals are best performed with their mastery.

5.3 Methods of Trance

In the *Disciple's Guide*, the simple and basic method of trance has been extensively covered as well as mechanisms involved and the

---

11   See *Initiation into Hermetics* by Franz Bardon – p. 97 - 98

necessity of various levels of trance used in the practice of ritual magick.

Trance can be deliberately self-induced or occur spontaneously. The magician is concerned with the deliberate assumption of a power trance, which can be as weak or strong as desired.

The strong trance state assists in the process of godhead assumption, scrying and astral projection. However, it can interfere with normal functioning, such as merely walking around, manipulating tools and reciting ritual verbiage or intoning incantations. Therefore, a weakened trance is the usual mind-state of a practicing ritual magician.

Competent magick is best performed as if in a dream state, with just enough mental clarity and focus to execute the elaborate rites without error or confusion. During this state, the mind is deep within and immersed in the domain of Spirit so that visions, images and subtle spiritual occurrences are perceptible and sensible. This mental state represents a delicate balance, only achievable after mastering techniques of self-hypnosis and trance by a continuous effort and practice.

Trance is achieved deliberately by first performing the basic meditation session, then by using the mechanisms of deliberately and intensively focusing the attention of the senses on a single object or phenomenon, such as a yantra, mantra, or the inhalation and exhalation of the breath. Deeper and more profound trance states may be experienced by increase the intensity and prolonging the effort. Attainment of the trance state is required to perform rituals, assume godheads or gain visions.

In this state of trance, the conceptual world of magick and its symbolic components become real and profoundly meaningful to the magician, who is at the center of its manifestation. The assumption of the trance state by the magician is deliberate and disciplined, and the images and concepts projected therein resonate in a powerful and deeply symbolic manner.

This is the essential mind state that makes the experience of magick seem real to the rational faculties of the magician. The unconscious mind has become temporarily superimposed over the conscious perception of reality, and the mundane world has become elevated to the level of the spiritual world through the altered perceptions of the five senses. This is so because we are normally unaware that the unconscious mind contains everything that we are as sentient egocentric beings, including our Higher Self (the God Within) and our connection to the superconscious domain of non-duality.

5.3.1 Trance Induction

There are a few additional variations on the technique of trance that are important enough to relate to intermediate students of magick. The first method involves the gaining a deep state of trance. This is accomplished by performing one of the two methods of either mantra or mandala for as long as it takes to assume the deepest trance that one is capable of assuming.

Begin this regimen not simply to quiet the mind, but to seemingly erase the mind altogether. The visualization used to gain this deeper state of trance is to imagine one's body falling slowly down a long dark tunnel into a great black void of nothingness. There is little fear since the sensation of falling is gentle and there is little that attracts the attention of the mind since all is uniformly dark. By eliminating and removing all other miscellaneous images and thoughts from the mind, a complete wakeful blankness can be achieved. This is an excellent state of mind for the seeking of a vision or for scrying into a crystal ball.

Another excellent method of deepening the trance state is to stare fixedly at a point of light projected on to a wall in a darkened room. Sometimes a single candle can be used if the air in the room is calm and the flame does not flicker much. You should stare fixedly at the spot of light, seeking what is beyond it, as if it were a porthole instead of just a point of light. After a period of time spent staring in this manner, you will begin to see past the point of light, and a whole world will open up to inner sight.

I particularly enjoy this type of trance sitting comfortably outside and staring at the full moon. After a period of time in my experience with this method, it seemed as if there was a dark spot on the surface of the moon, which opened up to reveal a luminous ring surrounded by darkness. I saw luminous lines of light shoot out from this opening and form a web of light, connecting everything in the sky and earth to it. It was quite an amazing visual experience, and one that was the product of a deep trance state.

The third method is where you think of a mental image and through the imagination, project it onto the outer world. This is often best achieved initially when the surrounding level of light is low, such as during the evening or very early morning. The greater the intensity of the affirmation that one is "seeing" this thing in one's normal field of reality, the more it seems to be real. This kind of reality projection can become so powerful that you can project things and objects that others can see - a kind of shared hallucination. Care should be taken with this technique, since if one too often sees what is not there, it could interfere with normal conscious functioning - of course.

The prior three techniques of trance induction all use the method of focused attention previously shared. Yet each technique creates a different mind-state. The visualization technique is a method of autohypnosis, used extensively by experts to deepen the trance state. The focused-awareness technique is used wherever you need to get a greater effect out of a mind-altering procedure, and it is this increased intensity or resonance that causes the enhancement. The trance internalization technique is the method used for the preparation of guided visualization and skrying (crystal gazing). The projection of images from the inner mind upon a visualized screen allows for the occurrence of clairvoyance, which is an important divination tool for the practicing magician.

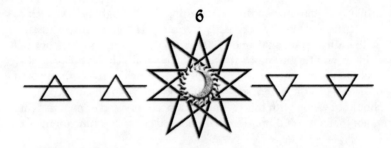

6

Magickal Topology (Sacred Space)

We live in a world that is continuously changing and defined by scientific achievements and discoveries. We know that angels don't live in the clouds playing harps and that hell is not in the infernal regions somewhere under the earth. All of the fantastic spirits, marvelous creatures and mythic landscapes that were once assumed to be in the undiscovered parts of the earth and sky are merely metaphors – symbolic products of the mind influenced by transcendental states of consciousness. The marvelous and fantastic phenomena of old have become something pushed into the distant vistas of the ultimate unknown limits of the cosmos.

Projecting the fabulous into the realm of science fiction and fantasy, we stand at a vast threshold within ourselves realizing that the strange mythic landscapes, spirits and legendary creatures are things of the deep mind. Entering therein, we discover the true nature of the World of Spirit. We seek not the mythopoetic worlds of Dante and Milton, but instead approach the domain and context of Spirit as being something that is found in the deepest recesses of the mind and soul of mankind, discovered and unleashed only as the higher and greater strata of consciousness become released in the individual seeker.

World of Spirit

This World of Spirit is the context for spiritual phenomena in magick. This is the reason why magickal rituals are performed in sacred space – to emulate the domain wherein magick exists. Magick doesn't work in a vacuum; it has a domain, a place where magickal phenomena are logical and explicable. However, that place is timeless, and it is both everywhere and nowhere. Magick also comes from within magicians - it is the heart and soul of their creativity, and this state is achieved by continual exposure to the World of Spirit.

We can attempt to conceptualize the domain of magick, making all kinds of varying and unique models, occult structures and diagrams, but they all fail to truly represent that world. They are only intellectual guides and not to be taken literally. However, throughout history the use of models has been a persistent practice and theme in most systems of magick. These models and their associated lore were used to depict the various underworld domains and celestial spheres in such a manner to assist the magician in determining where all the hierarchy of spirits resided. This was done because knowing where a spirit resided assisted the magician in contacting that spirit, since knowing its name and domain wholly identified it, making it accessible and intelligible.

Language fails to describe this spiritual world, and so do all conceptual maps, diagrams, and all theories about Spirit in general. The World of Spirit is entered directly through the techniques of mind control and through an immersion in symbols of transformation. The right combination of tools and techniques opens up the spirit world, revealing inner mysteries. A magician uses diagrams and models of the spirit world almost as a kind of talisman rather than a map, since they act as a means of forging a magickal link or alignment with that place.

Stated simply, the Domain of Spirit is the Other Side, the place of darkness, shadows and the unknown. It creates the duality of spirit and matter within our world, but it is accurately defined as being non-dual, a place of union and at-one-ment. This is, indeed, a paradox and a mystery. Since the spirit world is defined as being a wholeness of non-dual unity, then one can easily see why any model or description would fall far short.

How can anyone describe this state of union, or make multiple things or places from something that is implicitly one? The magician accomplishes this task by conceptualizing the spirit world as made up of a multitude of interlocking arrays through a model called the Inner Planes.

Models of the Inner Planes & Qabbalah

The Inner Planes of the Domain of Spirit are conceptualized in a Pythagorean manner, and depicted as tables or arrays, where there are distinct facet like cells, each a world unto itself, arranged together as various expressions of a unified symbolic hierarchy. They are a symbolic matrix, symbolizing worlds within worlds within worlds. These symbols in the matrix consist of the sacred symbologies of the deeper self (symbols of transformation), which are the four elements and spirit, planetary archetypes, zodiacal archetypes and various spiritual and cosmic spiritual hierarchies that combine together to formulate such systems as Astrology, Geomancy, the Tarot, Ritual Magick and the Qabbalah - or any other spiritual metaphysical system.

The domains of the Inner Planes are virtually limitless points of numinous transformation. All of these domains are found within the ground unconscious where they have their origin. However, they become an essential part of the emergent unconsciousness when they are activated, becoming a force that profoundly and permanently transforms the magician.

It is for this reason that the magician enters into these domains and makes contact with various spiritual entities contained therein. It is through this alignment, and a continual state of transformation and initiation, where complete enlightenment is achieved.

The basic structure of the Inner Planes consists of the seven planes of classical occultism, which has been distilled from theosophy and eastern metaphysical traditions.[12]

However, the Qabbalistic system defines the inner planes using a system of four divisions comparable to the four Elements or the Divine Tetrad. These four planes have been loosely defined in our culture as consisting of body, soul, mind and spirit.

In the Qabbalah[13], the body is associated with what is called the animal soul of humanity, containing all of the bodily needs and autonomic physical processes (Nephesch). Higher up is the volatile or emotional identity, the petty ego (Ruach, taken from Hebrew for breath or animating principle). The Ruach and Nephesch function

---

[12] For more information on the seven planes, macrocosm, & microcosm, refer to *Disciple's Guide to Ritual Magick* by Frater Barrabbas

13   See *Garden of Pomegranates* by Israel Regardie – p. 94 -97

jointly to produce animate and somewhat self-conscious beings, which would be all of the fauna and some of the flora of the material world. Lower forms of life just consist of Nephesch.

In the Qabbalah, humanity has the unique quality of possessing a self-conscious mind (Neschamah). Neschamah could also be considered the lower spirit or higher aspect of the true egoic self. Since the Qabbalah lacks a concept for the mind, we might consider this higher self as the unique conscious mind of the individual.

Corresponding to the indestructible individual spirit, which is above mind and body, would be what the Qabbalah calls the unique and true self (Yechidah), which is just slightly beyond the material definition of a person or being. The Yechidah would function as a person's individual spirit, and beyond even that would be the ever present godhead of that individual (Zureh), the Bornless (Headless) One or Atman.

Of all of the forms that make up a human being, only the Zureh is uncreated and eternal, existing in the greater cosmos of consciousness and wrapped up within its core as the body of the Union of All Being. It never ventures forth to participate in manifestation, and remains pure and inviolate.

The four parts of the soul would also compare to the four Worlds of the Qabbalah, which are Assiah, Yetzirah, Briah and Atziluth. These are ordered from the lowest world of material existence to the highest, which is the manifestation of the One as the Unified Godhead.

The four worlds represent the layers of spiritual emanation beginning with the One, then progressing and multiplying into the many, and eventually distilling into the myriad souls of all sentient life and their corporeal existence. The four Qabbalistic worlds represent the levels or boundaries of spiritual beings and their domains. The first world is the domain of the Unified Godhead (World of Origins: Archetypes, Aspects of Deity, Holism, Non-duality), the second, the domain of Archangels (World of Creation: Demigods, Emissaries, Active Principals), the third, the Angelic (World of Formation: Avatars, Bodhisatvas, Divine Ancestors, Guardian Spirits), and the fourth, the Heroic or Mundane (World of Expression: Heros, Heroines, Great Teachers and Thinkers, Initiates, the Greater Soul of Humanity).

The Tree of Life consists of Pathways and Primary Archetypes (Sephiroth), and is the archetypal model of the World

Tree, the conduit between heaven and earth, which contains all of the spiritual emitters and serpentine pathways of the descending and arising waves of the emanations of the Deity. The Tree of Life is both a model of the involution of Deity, manifesting itself from its essence into infinite forms, and it is a model of the evolution of human consciousness, revealing the mysterious and circuitous path back to the union of all being.

These ten Sephiroth and twenty-two paths are cast through the prism of the four Qabbalistic Worlds, causing there to be four Tree of Life models, one stacked on top of the other, as they exist separately and in each of the four Worlds. For instance, there is a Netzach of Assiah, and there is a Netzach of Atziluth, each representing a different order of magnitude of consciousness, but all still included within the definition of Netzach as a whole. To understand the ten Sephiroth, one must realize them as being expressed as a composite of four levels, which is the manner that they are presented in William Grey's book, *The Ladder of Lights*.

The merging of the Four Worlds and the Ten Sephiroth produces an array of 40 Spiritual Domains or Divine Worlds. Additionally, one can easily superimpose the forty cards of the Naibs of the Lesser Arcana of the Tarot (Ace to 10 of each Suit) upon the 40 Spiritual Domains of the Qabbalah. This becomes a powerful tool for defining those worlds in greater detail. The 40 Spiritual Domains are also one of the models of the Inner Planes of the Magician.

Inner Planes and the Domains of Higher Consciousness

We can see a parallel between the parts of the human soul, the domains of conscious development, and the Inner Planes. All three systems are intertwined in the practice of ritual magick.

In the ancient Egyptian theological system there were seven parts of the soul. Although this system was archaic and contained contradictions and duplications, it could be, by merit of the number seven, compared to the seven planets of the ancients. From this set of correspondences is derived a planetary system of the seven parts of the soul and also seven domains of spirituality, comparable to the Theosophical model of the Seven Rays, and other systems ruled by the number seven.

From the seven planets are derived two magickal arrays of symbols - the twenty-eight planetary talismans (combining planet and element - example: Mars of Fire), and the forty-nine binary planetary intelligences (combining planet and planet - Enochian Bonarum - example: Venus of Sun). There are also seven chakras in the eastern system of Kundalini Yoga, which could also be used to develop a system of Inner Planes.

Additionally, there are tables of symbolic correspondences based on a combination of element, planet, and even zodiacal qualities, as well as lists and qualities of deities and their emissaries, and a host of other information, arrayed against the 32 paths and Sephiroth of the Qabbalah. From these various tables of correspondences are derived the many worlds of the Inner Planes, all of which the magician seeks to encounter and experience at some point in one's magickal and spiritual journey.

If we propose seven levels of consciousness, with the first level consisting of the four levels of childhood development, which are the pleromatic, uroboric, typhonic, and membership-self levels, and the next six consisting of Mental Egoic, Centauric, Lower and Higher Subtle, and Lower and Higher Causal, then we would have a seven level model of consciousness that would represent the actual spectrum of human consciousness.[14] The domains of the Inner Planes would be found within each of those levels, but would be richer and more profound in the higher strata of consciousness. In the Subtle and Causal levels of consciousness, the Inner Planes residing there would contain all of the entities and symbologies that could trigger those higher states of consciousness in the one who beheld them, causing powerful mental transformations and emanating awesome transcendental phenomena.

It is for this reason that magicians seek out these higher domains, entering them to reveal the spiritual beings residing therein. Master magicians have learned to enter into the domains of the Inner Planes as part of their basic magickal discipline. The performance of many ritual operations allows for continuous access to the inner planes and the exposure to many profound transformations.

A System of spiritual hierarchies are developed, not to worship or edify those entities, but as a map and a means to contact each and every one of them through invocation, evocation, alignment, skrying and astral projection. In this way a magician learns to ride the planes of higher consciousness, and to realize

---

[14] See *Disciple's Guide to Ritual Magick* by Frater Barrabbas, section 3.5 - pp. 76 – 81 for levels of conscious development.

those higher levels of being within ones own normal conscious mind and mundane world. This methodology is called the "Golden Path", and is part of a new system of magick called Archeomancy. Even though it is based on an ancient Shamanic methodology - to follow the ghost roads of our ancestors into the realms of myth and magick -- The purpose of such a path is personal enlightenment and world transformation.

The one thing that bridges all of these various levels of models for the Inner Planes is the central point where all worlds and entities converge and merge into oneness. That central point has vertical levels but no horizontal ones. It is divided into three domains. The macrocosm is the greater domain of that central point; within it is found the microcosm, and also the mesocosm.

These three domains are coexistent, and act as analogues of each other. The macrocosm represents the most symbolic and abstract, and the microcosm the most tangible and least abstract. This is an analogy of the differences between something that is wholly spiritual and something that is wholly physical. For instance, the difference between the occult qualities associated with an emerald (its abstract significance) and the physical gemstone itself. The physical world is, in this fashion, symbolized and reflected by the spiritual.

The mesocosm is in the middle of these two worlds, where physical things represent or symbolize metaphysical ideas. Such a place would be realized as the temple or grove of the magician.

The bridge between worlds is variously symbolized by the World Tree, the Ladder of Lights, or Pylon of Heaven, and is the place where the powers of the macrocosm interchange with the powers of the microcosm. Certain tools and devices make this bridge accessible. In the magick circle, the place of convergence is the middle point. It's the place where magicians cause thought to become form and form to become a sacrament, to the greater good blessing of themselves, and ultimately, humanity itself. The center of the circle is where the pylon between heaven and earth is situated. It is used to anchor the pyramid of power and the self-containing vortex, and to ride the planes upwards and downwards. It is the one place where like is unto like, drawn together in a holistic web where everything is connected, and therefore, one.

Throughout the Inner Planes of the higher strata of consciousness exists the presence of Spirit. Spirit is union - the fusion of all consciousness into the One. It is also a mystery, since it is completely paradoxical to all rational thought.

Spirit is integral to consciousness and found wherever there is a mind and a soul. Spirit is the state of being that is trans-temporal - beyond all space and time, trans-egoic - beyond all self-definitions, transcendental, non-dual, infinite and essential.

Inner Planes and the Western Magickal Tradition

The Western Magickal tradition defines a number of systems of the Inner Planes. If we keep in mind that these various different worlds are nothing more than symbolic matrices or arrays of tables of correspondences, then we will have the key to all advanced magick. The adept magician is one who actively travels to and traffics with these various Inner Plane domains. The various ritual workings part of one's repertoire are rites allowing emmersion and alignment with these worlds. These tables of correspondences are drawn from elemental, planetary, astrological, the Tarot, ceremonial magickal, religious theological and Qabbalistic systems, and they represent the worlds of magick and the entities who populate it.

Following is an illustrated table of the various systems of correspondences that are used in the practice of ritual magick.

Systems of the Inner Planes - Archetypal and Symbolic Mappings of the Spiritual Domain

Magickal System	Symbolic Sources	Numeric System	Description of Inner Planes
Elemental Lunar Magick	Elemental - Divine Tetrad	4 x 4	16 Elemental Kingdoms
Talismanic Magick	Planetary - Talismans	7 x 4	28 Lunar Mansions
Lesser Theurgy	Binary Planetary Talismans	7 x 7	49 Bonarum - Heptarchia Mystica
Greater Theurgy	Zodiacal - Elemental	9 x 4	36 Decans - 72 Quniarians - enclosed within 12 Holy Houses.
Solar Underworld Ordeal	Tarot - Greater Arcana	22	22 Gateways of the Cycle of Initiation
Enochian Visionary Ordeals	Tarot - Lesser Arcana	14 x 4	56 Dominions of the Aethyrs
Archeomancy of the 40 Worlds	Qabbalah - Lesser Arcana	10 x 4	40 Qabbalistic Worlds - 40 Qualified Powers - Great Nested Hierarchy
Spiritual Archeomancy	Qabbalah - Greater Arcana	18	18 Qabbalistic Dimensions

The Inner Plane systems listed in the table above are ordered based on the level of magickal ability and competence it takes to master them. For example, the Enochian Ordeals are far more difficult and complicated to perform than the practice of Elemental Lunar Magick, yet both systems produce profound effects on the material plane. The former magickal system requires a greater depth and development to practice its magickal rites than the latter, and the adept who can perform the Enochian Ordeals can easily perform Elemental Lunar magick. It is said that the master magician is one who practices magick on all levels, and is flexible enough to one moment perform a very complicated and scripted ritual working, and the other moment, engage in spontaneous ritual making, using no scripts whatsoever.

The various analogues to these systems of magick are found in the mescocosm of the magick temple or grove. The magick circle, which exists in some form in both places of ritual operation, can be divided into numerous structures that are used to express complex rituals. There are eleven basic points in the magick circle, if one counts the four Watchtower, Angles, and the Ultra-point, Infra-point, and the Meso-point. The Watchtowers and Angles are used to work with the Elementals, and the Septagram and Eneagram (Decagram) Devices (situated in the center of the magick circle) are used to work with the Planets and the Qabbalah. The Gateway Keys and the double gateway of the Underworld Cycle assists in the rites of path working, as does the cross-roads and alternative gateways. The circle can be divided into as many as twelve nodes using the directions of the winds, and the circle itself guides all circumambulations, both deocil and widdershins, and inward and outward spirals. The charcoal, herbs, lamps, magickal tools, and furniture assist in establishing the magickal topology, as do the sigils, talismans, amulets, and various magickal diagrams and decorations, and the flora and fauna if the place is a grove.

In conclusion, we can see that all of these different dynamic and powerful systems of magick and the Inner Planes function together as the context and topology of ritual magick. Traveling into other worlds or domains has always been the preoccupation of the magician. However, in the present age we know these domains as models of the super-symbolic reality, the archetypal and symbolic core of the mind - that which gives the world its meaningfulness and intrinsic values of truth.

The affect of the other worlds of the Inner Planes on this world is produced by the emanation of transcendental or supernatural powers that alter and change it profoundly. It's the magick of Spirit impacting the mundane world and permanently changing it.

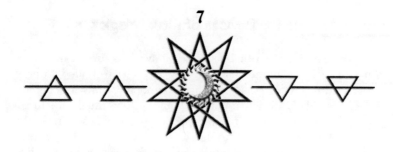

Magickal Ritual Structures

7.1 Introduction

Magickal rituals consist of specific components (actions and symbols), ordered in such a way as to represent an underlying theme or intention. The method of ordering these components produces a seamless and elegant ritual structure.

Prior to selecting and ordering ritual components, it is necessary to understand them with regards to their use and function. The components of a ritual are rituals unto themselves and the isolated actions of manipulating tools to form ritual patterns and draw devices are effective means of projecting magickal powers. Analyzing each of the primary ritual structures gives us an understanding of their symbolic content and how they are used in ritual magick.

Ritual structures consist of five basic geometric ritual categories that give meaning and structure to a ritual working. These five categories are defined in their basic form as the ritual structures of the midpoint, the pylon, the pyramid, the sphere and the spiral.[15]

Each of these actions, symbols and structures can function independently as a magickal ritual or "spell". When they are drawn together into a larger ritual structure, the potency of the magickal effect is significantly multiplied. It is for this reason that magicians artfully combine various components to form more effective, significant and sharply defined rituals.

---

[15] See section 7.3.4 on the Five Categories of Symbolic Alignment

7.2 The Devices of Ritual Magick

The possible range of ritual actions and symbols (devices) used in ritual magick are numerous, but they have been limited to only those used in this work. These ritual components consist of certain devices (symbols drawn in the air) and actual ritual structures. These devices are the spiral, the pentagram, the Rose Cross, the Rose Ankh, the Hexagram, the asanas and symbolic gestures (mudras). Rituals also incorporate visualization techniques that give form and substance to the symbolic images of ritual magick.

Since the detailed information about the devices of the Spiral, Pentagram and Cross have been extensively covered in the book, the *Disciple's Guide*, they will not be readdressed here.[16]

7.2.1 The Magick Hexagram

The magick Hexagram consists of the joining of two equilateral triangles to form a six-pointed star. This signifies that the whole is greater than the sum of its parts. The upright triangle represents the masculine forces of Fire, the inverted triangle the feminine forces of Water. Joined together they signify the union of Light and Darkness, masculine and feminine, to form a third quality, Union. Thus the Hexagram represents the Union of Being as the ultimate state symbolizing the Deity. The Hexagram represents the state of spiritual perfection that the magician seeks to know and express.

In the Golden Dawn tradition, the Hexagram was used to invoke the Seven Planetary Intelligences, with each point of the six-rayed star signifying six of these planets. The seventh planet, the Sun, was expressed through the combination of the six planets. Present day magicians replace the Hexagram with the Septagram (or Heptagram) for the invoking of Planetary Intelligences. The reason being is that the Septagram has a point for each of the seven planets and does not require any artifice to draw the invoking pattern for the Sun or any other planet. Although the Septagram is more difficult to draw in the air than the Hexagram, this problem can be resolved by using a specific septagrammic talisman with the planetary positions indicated for tracing of the planetary invoking patterns.

---

16   See *Disciple's Guide to Ritual Magick* by Frater Barrabbas – p. 149 - 163

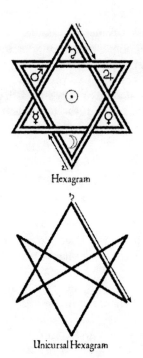

Hexagram

Unicursal Hexagram

HEXAGRAM
AS SYMBOL OF UNION

The magician uses the Hexagram to unify the other structures in a ritual simply by drawing it in the center of the circle, at the zenith or Ultrapoint. Therein, the Hexagram represents the magician's Higher Self as the Bornless One (God/dess Within). Once it is drawn, the Hexagram will immediately cause a synthesis of all prior energies, establishing a whole new and higher level of expression. Therefore, the Hexagram symbolizes the fusion of all prior magickal structures into union, such as the joining of archetypal male and female to create a synthesis, generating a unified field of pure Spirit.

A Hexagram can be drawn as either two distinct triangles that are superimposed, or as a continuous linear tracing, using a variant of the Hexagram called the Unicursal Hexagram. When drawing the double-triangle variant, the starting point is not important unless each of the points represents a specific Planetary Intelligence. However, one usually starts at the top point (Saturn) and proceeds clockwise when using the Unicursal Hexagram. Another method is to draw the upright triangle starting at its top point and proceeding clockwise, then drawing the inverted triangle starting at its bottom point (Moon) and proceeding clockwise to complete the double triangle of the Hexagram.

7.2.2 Asanas and Mudras

The asanas of the body, the gestures of the hands (mudras) and the position of the arms all represent specific symbolic expressions that have a special meaning when performed in the context of a magick circle. One could state that every body posture or gesture affected during a magick ritual is significant, and because the magician is the central focus of the ritual, this concept must be held as true.

93

However, rather than tabulate a complex system of asanas and mudras, only a handful are used as a deliberate means of affecting ritual significance. The rest are incidental, denoting a spontaneous expression of ritual action. The expression of ritual action should be considered theatrical and the many movements and postures that the magician may perform represent techniques to directly communicate the essential and internal meaning of the ritual.

In this book we will be considering only a few mudras as significant and deliberately symbolic, and leave the rest to the taste and imagination of the practicing magician.

The Osiris Position

Stand straight, legs together, but with the head tilted down, the arms are folded and crossed over your heart and the hands are in a fist, resting on the chest.

The hands can also be held unfolded with the open palms resting almost upon the shoulders without changing the meaning of the posture.

This asana signifies solidity, centeredness and completion. It also represents the Egyptian God Osiris as he attained the state of triumphant restoration and resurrection. This posture was taken from Golden Dawn lore.

The Cross Position

Stand straight, arms held out to either side of your body, parallel to the ground. Hands are held open, palms facing out and the head is directed forward.

This position signifies the human condition of being the mediation of both spirit and matter through the fusion of mind and soul (emotions). This symbolizes that humanity exists as the cross-roads between the Absolute Spirit and the world of manifestation.

The Mantle of Glory

Assume the asana of the Cross position for a moment, then proceed to connect the body chakras of the forehead, genitals, right shoulder, left shoulder and the heart with the right hand.

The resultant structure draws the chakras together into the figure of a cross, representing the spiritual body of light superimposed upon the physical body. This posture represents the magician as being physically warded from any potential harm either by the magician's unconscious mind or by the intentions of other magicians.

The Star Position

Stand with both legs spread apart, arms are held out, parallel to the ground and the palms held open and facing out, as in the Cross position. The head is also directed forward.

This position signifies the mastery of the Spirit, as directed by the mind and the will, over the four Elements. The Star position also signifies the ascension of the human spirit as it proceeds through the process of transformation and evolution.

The Ascension Gesture

Stand straight, with both legs together and the arms at your sides. Bend over at the waist and reach down with the hands to touch your feet.

Draw in the forces of the Earth from the feet, and then slowly draw this force up the body to the heart, resuming an upright posture.

Connect with the force centered in the heart by holding your hands over it and then projects it up over the head by raising your arms up and apart, forming a "V" with the hands each held in a fist.

This gesture signifies the ascending power of the individual having achieved the exaltation of spiritual union. The "V" formed by the arms stands for personal victory over all adversities.

The Assumption Gesture

After having performed the Ascension gesture with the arms raised up and apart in the form of a "V," slowly lower the arms to rest at the sides of your body.

Slowly position the hands folded over your heart with the hands open and the palms overlapping the chest, thus drawing the energy produced from the Ascension gesture down to center in the heart.

This gesture signifies that the state of the exaltation of Spiritual Union has been brought down to the center of one's being, therein having a profound influence on the course of daily life.

The Projection Gesture

Stand straight, with the feet together and arms at your sides. Then take the right foot and step forward while reaching forward with both arms and bending the body forward.

The fingers of the hands are extended as if groping in the darkness, and the arms are parallel to the head that is held looking down at the ground as if to negotiate the way forward.

At the moment of complete extension, exhale forcefully.

This gesture is analogous to the Golden Dawn gesture of the Sign of Horus and it signifies the projection of power through the body of the magician into the world at large. It also symbolizes the seeker groping in the darkness, seeking the light by the power of one's own will.

The Opening and Closing Portal Gestures

Stand before an imagined veil that separates you from the World of the Spirit. Then through the artifice of mime, open the veil slowly and with profound tension as if there were a great resistance.

This gesture is identical to the actual movements required to open a real curtain; the hands grasping the edges of the curtain seams, and then slowly pulling them apart to reveal what is obscured behind them.

Exhale profoundly as the veil is pulled open drawing the light and majesty revealed into your body.

The Closing Portal gesture is the opposite of the Opening Portal gesture: Stand before the opened veil, and take the opposing seams on either side of your body with your hands, drawing them together, causing the open hands to clap together as they meet in the closing of the veil.

This action is followed with the drawing of an Equal Arm Cross over the seams, thus sealing the closure.

The Opening and Closing Portal gestures represent the opening and closing of the veil that separates different levels of energy and states of being, the subsequent entering and exiting represents the passage between worlds and states of consciousness. This gesture is used with the ritual pattern of the Gate.

The Signs of the Four Elements and Spirit

The signs of the four Elements and Spirit are taken from the traditional Golden Dawn signs of the four grades of initiation. Illustrations and their accompanied directions may be found in the following three books: *The Golden Dawn, Book II*, by Israel Regardie; *Liber O, The Equinox, Volume 1*, edited by Aleister Crowley; and *Magick in Theory and Practice*, by Magister Therion (Aleister Crowley). Each of these signs has a particular gesture and these can be quickly mentioned.

Sign of Fire

The gesture for Fire is performed with the hands held out, the fingers of each hand held together, pointing up, palms flat, thumbs extended and the index and thumbs of each hand are touching to form an upright triangle of Fire. This mudra is held over the head.

Sign of Water

The gesture for Water is similar to Fire except that the finger tips are held pointing down, forming an inverted triangle. This mudra is held at waist level.

Sign of Air

The gesture for Air is the sign of the Egyptian God Shu, supporting the Sky with his arms. The gesture consists of holding the arms out and bent 90 degrees at the elbows, with the hands extended out and the palms facing up.

Sign of Earth

The gesture for Earth consists of emulating the sign of the aphorism "as above, so below," where the magician stands straight with the right arm held up at 45-degree angle and the left arm down at a 45-degree angle. The index finger of the right hand points to heaven and the index finger of the left hand points to the ground.

Sign of Spirit

The gesture for Spirit is the same as the Osiris position.

Other Postures

Additional postures that can assume major significance are the positions of kneeling, standing, sitting and lying down. There are also others of lesser significance that may appear. The method of determining their meaning is to examine the context in which they appear in a ritual and to judge their dramatic effect. This methodology will also assist the student in determining the significance of any posture, gesture or mudra in a ritual. All rituals are context sensitive and their actions derive significance through contrast with other actions.

7.3 The Structures of Ritual Magick

7.3.1 Visualization

One of the most important tools that a magician can wield is visualization. The methodology actually embraces several techniques, all of which incorporate the use of suggestion to stimulate the imagination. Visual imagination is the principal component of visualization, without it a magician will find these techniques very difficult to perform. In fact, the lack of this ability will make it challenging for a magician to practice any form of magick.

Not everyone has a vivid imagination, but most people create visions while they read or listen to stories. Images are often employed in teaching new concepts or complicated processes. It is within the power of most people to fantasize and imagine without any outside stimulus - such as daydreaming, visualizing pleasant thoughts or reliving memories. The techniques of visualization seek to harness that innate tendency to daydream and fantasize, and through structure and discipline, cause it to be forged into a formidable tool.

It has been demonstrated that through visualization one can gain some control over autonomic physiological processes. This is accomplished by creating a feedback loop connecting the body to the visual senses through some mechanism; this process is called biofeedback. However, occultists of every persuasion have used meditative forms of visualization for centuries to alter consciousness, contact the deeper psyche or even control bodily functions. It is in contacting the deeper psyche that a magician employs the techniques of visualization. The techniques are tailored to assist in transforming awareness and causing the unconscious Higher Mind to emerge.

Visualization, in its most simplistic state, is the act of controlling and focusing the mind's natural ability to fantasize. Controlling the imagination directs the attention to the manifestations of the deeper psyche. Most of the time when we fantasize, daydream or dream while sleeping, we pay little attention to what is transpiring in our minds, allowing for an almost formless kind of free association. Many people dream at night without remembering their dreams upon waking. But when we structure and imprint the natural visualization process, the conscious mind is suddenly open to what is being subtly communicated from the unconscious mind, and a mechanism of two-way communication is established.

The control of natural visualization occurs only when the magician deliberately exercises and practices it. This regimen should be on a daily basis. After a period of practice, this process becomes automatically available to the magician, enhancing the effectiveness of ritual magick. There are several techniques that the practicing magician can use to practice this ability, which may be incorporated into the preparation and practice of any magickal working. The first two techniques involve the visualization of specific colors (auras) in symbolic association with magickal energies and the visualization of lines of colored energy (tracers) being drawn in the air with the hands or magickal tools.

7.3.2 Visualization Techniques

Sensing Energies

The technique of visualizing magickal energies as colors begins with simply imagining a certain color and holding it in the mind for increasing periods of time. There is a corresponding symbolic quality for each color, and these are explored as one holds it in visualization. The first steps are done with the eyes closed, and then as the process becomes more controlled, the eyes are opened and the color is perceived as being superimposed over physical reality. Once this step is accomplished, the magician has learned the initial method of allowing imagination to project images upon reality, thus altering it. The symbolic quality of each color also evokes a response from the unconscious mind, thus allowing the visualization of colors to produce emotional and visual associations. The magician notes these observations, and builds a repertoire of colors that evoke certain emotions and images, becoming an individualized colorized palette of magickal powers.

Visualizing Tracers

The technique of visualizing tracers can be assisted with the use of a lighted stick of incense. The glowing end of the incense stick produces tracers when the stick is moved rapidly around. Certain patterns can be temporarily perceived when the stick is used to draw figures in the air, most notably magickal symbols such as Pentagrams, Spirals, or Crosses. The magician holds the tracer images in mentally so that the brief visual image is dimly perceived to continue after it has faded. This method is practiced until the image is seen not to fade at all but remains vivid and hanging in mid-air well after the actual image is gone. The magician then learns to perform the same process with an object that has no illumination, like a magick dagger, wand or sword, seeing the faint but clear energy patterns that these tools make when drawing figures in the air. They are best perceived imagined in different colors, denoting the different types of energies involved.

Practicing these techniques should be a regular part of one's magickal discipline. Learning to perceive energies and tracers, the lines of force and the color qualities of the energies that are generated assists the magician in better understanding the effects of the geometric ritual structures that are employed in various Grimoire. Also it increases the sense of the ritual at the level of magickal operations and therefore accentuates the capability of manipulating the subtle energies used in ritual magick. A magician who has not cultivated these two techniques will function blindly in ritual performance and experience.

Guided Meditation

Guided meditation consists of a symbolic narrative hypnotically spoken, following an intense period of meditation, self-centering, controlled breathing, mantra chanting and then deep trance (with the eyes closed). The narrative is read slowly and quietly with lengthy pauses between each passage, allowing the imagination to build up and the suggestive images implied until they have almost an opaque quality. The narrative is repeated at intervals until its essence has been fully absorbed into the unconscious mind where it is given greater depth and significance.

Environment Sensing/Scrying:

The final two techniques of visualization directly involve the use of creative visualization through visual trance. These two similar methods are known as environment sensing and skrying. Environment sensing is where magicians perform a sensory scan of their immediate environment in order to establish an alignment with it and open the self to outer psychic stimuli. In this manner, magicians control the power channeled through the temple or grove through their body. In this, the body becomes like a great sensitive wand and with the ability to directly perceive the magickal world-view.

Magicians create sensory fields around the body through creative visualization. This expands their awareness far beyond the five senses, opening up the visual mind to the reality of magick. The resultant feelings and sensations that are perceived through the body and the mind are used to interpret things that are hidden to the physical senses but exist in physical reality.

The technique of skrying involves the direct use of visual trance while focusing the eyes upon the magick mirror or crystal ball (shew stone). Skrying uses preselected suggestions as a form of inquiry, allowing for the formation of images, illusions and symbolic revelations. The images are always fleeting, so the skrier must always know how to lock into a significant image and allow it to slowly develop.

Another variation of skrying is astral projection. In astral projection, the focus of the trance is applied to the body. A suggestion of freeing up the Astral body from out of its physical container is used to gain a conscious egress into the Astral world.

Then the subject projects one's awareness completely into the Astral body of light. The experience proceeds with the magician functioning in the Astral body in the parallel Astral world and even beyond, into the vortex of the internal psychic reality of the World of the Spirit.

Following, you will find a series of exercises to facilitate these techniques of visualization. These exercises must be practiced regularly. Once accomplished, the aforementioned text will be much more informative.

Exercise 1 - Color Visualization

a.   Imagine a color with your eyes closed, sense its qualities in terms of feelings and thoughts and note any associations. You may use colored geometric shapes as models, which are gazed steadily upon and then visualized with the eyes closed. Begin with the primary colors, and then graduate to the complimentary colors.

b.   Imagine a color with the eyes open and practice seeing that color superimposed over physical objects. Begin by staring at a geometric diagram (a Yantra), then shift the gaze to a monochrome wall or flat surface. This should be accomplished in a dimly illuminated space. Then graduate to projecting visualized colors over varied and colored surfaces. Attempt to see the color of an object change in your mind to one that you choose.

c.   Walk outdoors in the daylight in a secluded place and attempt exercise 1b. Any degree of success will indicate that you have mastered this process.

Exercise 2 - Tracers and Lines of Force

a.   In a darkened room, use a burning stick of incense or a glowing punk to trace Spirals, Crosses, Pentagrams, Ankhs, Hexagrams and other shapes. Observe the natural tracers and try to focus on them and visualize their continued occurrence even after the actual visual effect has disappeared.

b.   Attempt exercise 2a again except with a non-illuminating object, like your hand or a magick tool such as a dagger or a wand. You should attempt this in a dimly lit room and the tracers should be faint but very readily perceived. The method of visualizing a nonilluminating object producing tracers is analogous to visualizing the etheric and auric fields of light that surround the body. Careful observation of another person in a dim room using the same technique will reveal this mystery.

c. Combining the techniques of visualizing tracers and colors, attempt to draw a Cross or an invoking Pentagram and project a color onto it, imbuing it with that quality. When drawing lines of force, imagine them having a luminous quality of color and resonating with the power associated with that color of light.

Exercise 3 - Guided Meditation

a. The Proper Meditation Session: Sit in a comfortable asana for thirty minutes to two hours. Begin the session with a centering exercise, then followed by a ten minute period of breath control (the fourfold breath method). After this is accomplished, begin to intone a mantra (using a very nasalized AUM sound) and continue to intone it for a five minute period. This is followed by contemplative silence for five minutes, while focusing the eyes on an inanimate object and staring until a trance state is established. This is done while continuing a very steady and restful breathing cycle. Then close your eyes and visualize a blank screen in your mind. This is the preparatory stage to experiencing a guided meditation.

b. Guided Narratives and Invocative Meditation: It is recommended that you first establish the preparatory mind state using the proper meditation session before embarking on a guided meditation. Then listen as the narrator slowly, quietly and with many pauses reads each section of a prepared guided meditation text. An example is the narration found in the Lunar Mystery of the *Disciple's Guide*, particularly the section about "Entering the Grail Chapel", and the "Lunar Mystery" tone poem.[17] After the narration is read at least two times, allow for a long period of silence for individual exploration and resolution. There may be soft music playing or even the monotonous beating

---

[17] See *Disciple's Guide to Ritual Magick*, by Frater Barrabbas, pp. 279 - 283

of a single drum (four beats per second). The narration and music may be taped previously to facilitate solitary visualization sessions. At the close of the guided meditation period, the narrator directs the other meditators to return to the ordinary waking world. The guided meditation is completed with another grounding exercise.

Exercise 4 – Sensor Fields and Exterior Trance

a. This exercise should be performed indoors and with no distractions. Establish a trance state, as described in Section 5.6.1 of this book (Trance Induction) aided with an initial period of meditation as a preparation. The trance state should be performed with the eyes open and in a standing posture. You begin by extending both hands and attempting to feel the subtle energies around you. When it produces the desired effects, you will be able to sense the room with your hands and your body in a new and different manner. For a more intense effect of body sensing, try closing your eyes.

b. Perform the above exercise outdoors in a secluded natural spot. You may partake of certain sacramental substances to aid the process if you wish, but they are not necessary. Wander around the landscape and attempt to sense a connection with each unique item encountered. The items that you focus on can be any natural objects such as rocks, trees, flowers, plants, streams, hills or valleys. You may alternate between having your eyes open and closed when in the act of sensing an object. After a period of time you should become quite aware of the interconnectedness of all the living and inanimate objects around you.

c. For an advanced form of the above two exercises, sit in a predetermined sacred space and draw lines of force from your body to various objects surrounding you. Attempting to feel the living qualities from the object whether it is animate or inanimate. As you draw a new line of force, the old line of force remains and adds to the background of the intensity of the newly felt connection. In this manner you will slowly create a web or network of connections through which you can sense and feel. Then sit very still and see if you can sense any minute change or occurrence in that sensory web.

Exercise 5 - Skrying and Projection

a. To accomplish the technique of Astral projection, I give reference to a few various written works that are better than a mere paragraph here. These contain important details required for a successful projection: Practical Astral Projection, by Yram; Art and Practice of Astral Projection, by Opheal; Astral Projection, by Oliver Fox, and The Projection of the Astral Body, by Sylvan Muldoon and Hereward Carrington.

b. The technique of skrying is begun with a thirty minute period of silent meditation, in preparation and establishment of the proper mental state. The skrying session will take some time to accomplish, so you should be seated before the crystal ball or skrying mirror in a very comfortable chair or pillow. Then, establish a deep trance with your attention focused intently upon the skrying mirror or crystal ball. The skrying surface will eventually appear to fade or become somewhat indistinct due to eye fatigue. This is the state in which a hypnotic suggestion can cause you to see images or visions. The question that you seek to have answered is quietly spoken, beginning as a whisper and diminishing until it is only thought. Your eyes are still gazing intently at the skrying surface, visualizing it becoming cloudy or smokey as the fog of the Inner Sight emerges. Then you should project a strong desire into it to learn the answer to your question, and this will penetrate the cloudy veil and cause a series of images to appear. It is upon this cloudy veil that the imagination is freely projected, causing an almost chaotic flow of free association.

c. When an image occurs that seems to be significant, you should focus upon it and lock it into your visualization trance state. The result of this fixation will cause an unconscious symbol to be held by both the conscious and unconscious minds, allowing a direct communication between them (a sort of handshake). The resultant images should be noted by an attendant scribe and then allowed to pass, to be replaced by others that will be judged as being important or not, and then held in the mind's eye if they are significant. The skryer can also use a hand-held digital recorder or some other kind of small recording device.

When the process is completed, the notation of significant images can be analyzed. Usually a very striking and coherent message is derived. You should understand that the unconscious mind speaks the language of symbols, and the images seen will have a cryptic quality but will reveal their mystery upon closer scrutiny. When the skrying session is completed, then the skryer should perform a grounding exercise as well as stretch and relax the body.

7.3.3 Anatomy of Ritual Structure & Design

Previously covered in this book are the components of magickal ritual, consisting of symbolic devices and ritual actions (archetypal expressions), used to express symbolic ideas. It is important to note, however, that how we organize a ritual is just as important as what it contains.

A ritual is not simply a string of actions and symbolic expressions without any order or form. One cannot randomly paste a series of ritual actions together, embellish them with the use of ritual devices, call it a ritual working, perform it and expect it to work.

Based upon vague and contradictory writings, some magicians seem to think it's appropriate to dispense with deliberate structures advocating a purely random approach to building rituals. Serious practitioners will insist that careful deliberation is the hallmark of successful ritual magick.

Ritual Patterns, Structures and Occult Ideals

The basic design of a ritual is its pattern. A ritual pattern consists of *ritual structures* that are joined together to express, in a paradigm, desire and intention. A ritual pattern is finite in its scope and function, but it can be used and re-used in a myriad of ways. Ritual structure is the basic part of a ritual pattern; and there can either be a few or many ritual structures used in the pattern.

A ritual structure is itself a symbol of magickal power and meaning, and therefore contains specific meta-symbols, *symbolic actions* and *archetypal expressions* brought together in a synthesis to express a single *occult ideal*.

One or more ritual actions combined together build up a ritual structure. In the past, a ritual structure would have been considered a distinct magickal spell, performed for a separate magickal effect – now they are grouped together to form larger aggregates. The ritual structure in turn expresses the occult ideal, which is the meaningful core of the ritual structure.

Symbolic devices, symbolic actions and archetypal expressions are the letters of the alphabet of a hypothetical language of ritual magick. They function together as meta-symbols, forming word-like aggregates.

We can use the analogy of language to understand the relationship between rituals, ritual patterns, structures and occult ideals. Ritual patterns are like the syntax of a language that organizes the words to form meaningful sentences, so ritual patterns organize ritual structures to form rituals. As words are used selectively to make sentences, the ritual structure is used to make up a completed ritual. Thus ritual structures are a modular and re-useable component of a ritual, just like words are in a sentence.

The relationship of the occult ideal to ritual structures is like the semantic meaning of words. In other words, occult ideals represent the meaning that a ritual structure possesses. Just like a sentence could be syntactically correct but also meaningless, it's important to consider that a ritual could also be meaningless unless the occult ideals fit the purpose or function of the ritual. However, occult ideals are more difficult to determine than the meaning of words in a sentence.

A ritual working is the highest structure, and in our analogy, it functions like a paragraph. A ritual working represents an organization of rituals to perform a specific purpose or task, such as a healing working, or a working to jump start one's career, or invoking a spirit to perform a specific task or answer specific questions.

An example: the components of a ritual structure include the actions of drawing the invoking pentagram in the air with the wand, intoning a letter of a magickal formula, expressing an associated spiritual belief or tenet, or summoning the imago of an Archangel.

The occult ideal associated with this ritual structure is the formula letter and the associated declaration. In other situations, the occult ideal may be implicit and unstated. Determining the occult ideal for a given ritual structure may not always be obvious, but it can be determined by examining all of the components of a ritual structure.

Sequentially performing this ritual structure, deocil, starting in the East, and proceeding to the four cardinal directions, and then to the center of the circle would produce a ritual pattern that would draw together various ritual structures to form a completed ritual.[18] Such a completed ritual could be used with other rituals to form a ritual working.

Nature of the Occult Ideal in Ritual

An occult ideal is drawn from a significant part of a body of beliefs (lore) about the nature of spirit, reality, being and the relationship between them (ontology). This body of lore represents the magician's practical magickal philosophy. The occult ideal is the smallest level of meaning in a ritual pattern so it functions as the semantic background or deep-structure in the language of magick.

The occult ideal that is expressed in the core of a ritual structure makes a profound statement that subtly affects the practicing magician's world-view, beliefs, and expectations. The occult ideal always consists of a synthesis of a basic symbolic archetype and its subjective value or sentiment, as determined by its context and definition. Therefore, to understand the beliefs and motivations of magicians, we need only to examine their rituals, specifically noting the declarative statements and symbolic actions.

Occult ideals can be categorized into five basic archetypal concepts. These categories group various types of ritual structures together that have a common significance. They are an obvious heuristic device that I have invented and represent a way of organizing ritual structures into a five different basic occult ideals.

The five categories of the occult ideals are simply stated as *identity, occurrence, polarity, alignment and resonance.* The five categories represent the five most basic ritual structures of the *point, pylon, pyramid, sphere, and the spiral.* They are used to assist in

---

[18] Such a ritual would form a power structure using the pyramid, whose base squares the circle. These would also contribute to the overall meaning and efficacy of the ritual.

determining the occult ideal for any given ritual structure, since this is not typically obvious.

However, they also represent the sequence of evolving spiritual emanations of the Deity unto the created world. And implicitly in reverse, they represent evolution of consciousness unto the Godhead. Occult ideals are signified as a specific quality of spiritual-consciousness (symbols of transformation), representing the most basic symbolic states in the domain of absolute consciousness. Occult ideals cannot be divorced from the states of consciousness that define them or their powers and meaningfulness become lost.

The five categories are built upon variations of the concept of the relationship between the Deity and the domain of the super-symbolic world. In this, through the processes of creation, Godhead as unity is multiplied into the many individual spiritual lights through the process of emanation.

Magicians take the role of the Deity and through the artifice of the all of the tools and techniques of ritual magick engage in the manipulation of the physical world. This is done in emulation of the Deity with whom one is in alignment.

Ritual Pattern as Occult Paradigm

Thus far, all of the symbolic devices and ritual actions we have covered are the symbolic components of a ritual structure. The ritual pattern, which draws together the various ritual actions and archetypal expressions (devices and ideals) that form the ritual structures, imparts a specific order and sequence to magickal events.

The order of ritual events expresses the theme and background of a ritual, telling its story. The ritual pattern is a sequence of ritual events, and may be depicted graphically like a storyboard utilized by animators and film makers. The pattern tells a story using the various Gods, Angels, Demons, Spirits and Mythic Beings as the cast of characters; the dialogue and actions represent the occult ideals and the interaction of the cast, the drama. The paradigm weaves all the elements together within a plot whose ultimate outcome is the magician's objective.

The art of ritual magick consists of two important ingredients: establishing the proper state of consciousness and performing a ritual that elegantly expresses the intention of the magician. When these two ingredients are perfectly blended, then ritual performance becomes an enactment of an actual psychic event that represents both that which is within the magician and that which is outside in the world.

The ritual structures of magick express powerful transformative occult ideals. On some level, the magician must fully realize these transformative occult ideals as such, and not block their effect through either fear or inhibition. Symbolic meaning can be directly experienced and understood only when the mind is sufficiently altered and not engaged in analyzing everything as it is happening. The symbolic reality of magick must become translated into the material and mental reality of the magician.

A successful performance of ritual therefore directly communicates with the magician's Higher Self (the God/dess Within). Through the inspiration of the Higher Self, the magician becomes self-directed and self-inspired, thus ascending the planes of consciousness to ever higher levels, ultimately to unite with the Deity. Then the magician returns to the world of humanity, filled with the inspiration of a transforming potency and having the will to use it as a world-transforming tool. This is the cycle of transformative initiation that occurs every time that a ritual is effectively performed. We will discuss this cycle later in this work.[19]

This is the exemplar of the magician's progress and the underworld circuit of transformative initiation. Through this process, the magician harnesses the dynamic polarity of the Macrocosm and the Microcosm. From that point, everything that is possible can be made actual through the expression of ritual.

Ritual Patterns and Unified Expressions

In order to introduce the greater details of ritual structure, it is important to establish the pattern that every ritual uses. We have already examined the pattern of rituals that generate magickal power and the two basic energy types, the cone of power and the vortex.

A ritual of empowerment is a simple ritual pattern because it consists only of three magickal actions:

> *Generating a magickal field of power through the symbolic enactment of sexual union
> * Imprinting that power with an intention

---

[19] See section 9

* Releasing it through exteriorization and resonance

The methods of generating magickal power and imprinting it have a great variety of expressions and techniques, and can be quite diverse. However, the ritual pattern of a complex ritual working usually uses an alternative climax, formulating a surrogate for exteriorization. There are the first two steps of the three defined above (symbolically generating power and imprinting it), and an alternative climactic step where the symbolic components of the ritual are restated as a unified expression.

The unified expression can be in the form of a simple synopsis or summary, or it can be expressed as a symbolic acronym. Unified expression is typically performed in the center of the magick circle, making it a symbolic amalgam of unity.

The use of a unified expression or synopsis is an important part of a ritual structure because it causes the flow of the ritual to be recursive (it ends where it begins), thus enabling it to be connected to other ritual structures that are performed serially as a complete ritual. The recursiveness of a ritual structure within a ritual emulates the recursive nature of consciousness itself.

A magickal ritual that is going to be used with other rituals usually has three basic magickal actions: manipulating magickal power; manipulating symbolic meaning; and expressing the uniform symbol of the ritual.

The manipulation of magickal power consists in the generation and imprinting of that power. The magickal action of exteriorization has been omitted because the power needs to be built up and conserved by a series of rituals and then unleashed at the very end. The manipulation of symbolic meaning is the part of a ritual pattern where the occult ideal is expressed by a combination of symbolic actions and archetypal expressions (declarations and incantations).

The final ritual in a complex ritual pattern has four parts. The first two steps of the final ritual are the same as the other rituals -- manipulation of magickal power and manipulation of symbolic meaning. The third step would be a summary of all previous rituals that is expressed in a single unified concept. The final ritual structure would be the exteriorization of the total accumulated energies.

The flow of magickal power through a ritual working is intensified and amplified through the recursiveness of the sequence of linked rituals that are a part of it. This magnifies the power and significance of the working until it is abruptly discharged using a technique of exteriorization.

Manipulation of Power, Symbols and Unity

The manipulation of power can consist of both the use of ritual structures of empowerment as well as exteriorization. The ritual structures of empowerment represent variations in the symbolic joining of the archetypal masculine and feminine polarities.

To begin the symbolic process of a rite, magicians use the ritual artifice of making a statement or declaring an intention, thus identifying the target or objective. One may use actual physical items associated with the object of desire as a link, or choose items that are analogous but entirely symbolic. The purpose of the ritual may be declared or it may be implied. The fact that the magician is performing a ritual might be the only purpose needed to justify the working (thus, "Ago ergo sum," I do, therefore I am).

The ritual structures of exteriorization consist of the actions of projecting the collected energy field through an ecstatic release (exteriorization as resonance and projection). The action of directing the force includes of the conscious process of focusing the energy and imprinting it with an intention. The action of resonance is the deliberate intensification of the ritual expression until ecstatic release is achieved. The manipulation of magickal power gives the magician clarity of purpose, decisiveness and inspiration to joyfully achieve the objective of the magickal working.

Manipulation of symbolic meaning is nothing more than the communication of the objective and purpose of the ritual, stated in the form of occult ideals. The raising of magickal power becomes an empty act without the purpose, intention, objective, and the unifying link that is provided by the symbolic expressions and manipulations performed by the magician. Intention is grounded in the magickal pattern (as the innate desire). It is only obliquely expressed because all the ritual actions are communicated symbolically. The intention may be couched in occult symbols that are obscure to the mind, but they produce the maximum impact upon the unconscious mind and within the spiritual world. The symbolic expression of the ritual intention is how the magickal symbolic link is derived.

The basic rule operating here is that magicians must express their intention symbolically at the highest level and in a language that is intelligible to that level of being (Spirit), thus establishing a (spiritual) link between the object and the intention. Therefore, the artifice of occult symbolic representation is used, and the magician manipulates these symbols as if they were the actual things that they represent. The magician does this because in the magickal mind-state, the symbols are directly associated with what they represent. The manipulation of these symbols unleashes a psychic effect that aids in the fulfillment of the ritual objective.[20]

In other words, the link is just a simplified expression of the magician's desire. This simplified expression configured as a phrase or mantra can be chanted continuously in an ever-increasing tempo, thus causing the latent field of magickal power in the circle to resonate with it (to be imprinted). The link can also be a sigil or symbolic diagram as well.

Symbolic components of the ritual may also be divided into an acronym consisting of a four-letter formula (i.e., a tetragrammaton) with each letter being expressed at each one of the four Watchtowers , four Angles or some other configuration.

The symbolic expression of the link could consist of the joining of these four letters into a single word, with the magician chanting this word as a symbol of unity. The direction that the magician would progress in performing these actions would be deosil (clockwise) to express the powers of manifestation, or widdershins (counterclockwise) to express the powers of liberation.

Through the use of these simple ritual structures, the magician is able to express the intent and the desire of the ritual, and also to imprint the magickal power with the symbolic expression of the magickal link.

A resultant field of meaning and power may be either exteriorized to impact the physical world or summarized as a unified expression so that another higher level of ritual artifice and power may be established.

How the concept of unity is expressed in a ritual is through the mechanism of a ritual synopsis. This is where all of the significant parts of the ritual are summarized at the end (the ending is the beginning).

A synopsis captures the whole and the essence of a ritual. It can even be used to form another synopsis that is performed at the end of a ritual working. A series of rituals in a ritual working would

---

[20] However, the associated mundane actions must always be accomplished as well in order for the ritual working to be successful.

each have a synopsis at their end, and then all of the synopses would be use to form a grand synopsis at the end of ritual working, thus tying all of the elements of the rituals and the ritual working together. A synopsis is the hook that allows rituals to be merged together. It can also represent the embodiment of the ritual intention as well.

The law of synergy states that the whole is greater than the sum of its parts, and therefore the ritual working has a greater effect than the independent serial expression of each of its component rituals. The ritual synopsis causes ritual components to be subjected to this rule; therefore it is integral to a complex magickal working.

7.3.4 Models of Consciousness

Magicians use models of consciousness and the inner planes to conceptualize magickal reality so it can be understood and operated upon. Magicians use models, analogies, diagrams and tables of correspondences extensively even though these structures are imperfect and useful only to a point. While these various devices would seem to be artificial and even absurd, they are symbolic approximations of the unknowable World of Spirit as perceived with a transcendental mental mind-state. In this state, the models, analogies, diagrams, and tables seem to come alive and respond to the magician's manipulations. Such devices are tools and not to be confused with what they represent.

The structure of the Seven planes of consciousness has already been covered and therefore the spectrum of consciousness has been mapped as it pertains to the individual. The structure of the Seven planes is the first model of consciousness that a magician learns in order to use and categorize the various interpenetrating worlds of matter, mind and spirit.

However, there are two additional models that assist the magician in conceptualizing the attributes of the Deity, how it relates to the cosmos and the individual, and how the individual relates to it. These similar models are the Ten Emanations of Divine Creation and the Magick Pyramid.

The ten emanations of divine creation are represented as a model of consciousness at a macrocosmic and microcosmic level, symbolized by the diagram of the Qabbalistic Tree of Life.

The magick pyramid represents the synthesis of the ten emanations and the seven planes, condensed into a pyramidal structure known to the followers of the Pythagorean philosophy as the divine Tetractys. The magick pyramid symbolizes the relationship of consciousness between the Deity and the individual being. It contains four definable levels within it, representing the fourfold World of the Spirit.

The divine Tetractys contains all ten emanations of the Deity as well as the seven planes of individual consciousness collapsed into four planes or levels. It is a model of the dynamic state of consciousness of the individual being because each person contains within them the seed of the infinite and unknowable source.

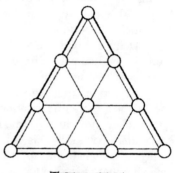

TETRACTYS

The structure of dynamic consciousness is hierarchical and pyramidal, and is integral to animate life. At the pyramid's summit, consciousness is perceived as holistic and indivisible. At its base, it is perceived in a granular fashion, representing the domain of individual conscious beings that are seemingly separate, but in fact are part of the greater whole.

The summit of the pyramid of consciousness is also the absolute level that contains all the prior levels, expressed only in a symbolic and unified expression. The summit is recursive (the end is the beginning), for it represents all of the prior levels in union. Because of the Law of Synergy, it is also a level of greater being unto itself.

Each individual represented at the base of the pyramid is recursively reflected in the holistic expression of the Absolute State. However, this process of recursiveness doesn't stop at that point. Human beings are also a holistic expression of a myriad of cells and chemical interactions, which somehow lend themselves to the generation of the mind, soul and spirit. Thus at each scale of being this holistic and pyramidal model is significant. The pyramidal model of consciousness represents both the integration of the Absolute State of Unity at its summit, and the separation of unique individual beings at its base, as well as the building up of all of the stages of life, from the most primitive to the most complex.

The difference between the Godhead and individual spirits is one of scale and not insurmountable (macrocosm vs. miscrocosm). This is easily understood when we examine the model of the magick pyramid.

The distinction between the autonomous human beings at the base, and the Unified Spirit of the Deity at the top is relative. They are also not based upon a difference of substance, since both the Deity and humanity are analogously structured. So the differences are actually illusory.

Deity contains all of the consciousness of individuals, and more. Individual beings have their own internal Godhead, and can access and become completely one with the Absolute level of Being simply by connecting with that inner Deity. To do this, one must change their egocentric definition of self and its relative boundaries, but that is not an insurmountable task. The maintenance of egocentric boundaries is essential to individual survival, so changing them is not a simple matter. The ego itself can fool us into believing that the individual is autonomous and the *summum bonum* of all aspiration. The method of changing one's definition of self and extending its boundaries is accomplished through continuous self-transformation, a state called the Transcendental Process.

Transcendental Process is activated though the assumption of an elevated state of consciousness, representing a major change in one's level of awareness. Associating higher levels of consciousness with a greater awareness of the spiritual dimension of being, the magician transcends the boundaries of self. This is accomplished by using methods to trick the mind into expanding the definition of the self, causing it to be momentarily divorced from the body-centric ego and its narrow focus.

Consciousness consists of a pyramidal cyclic progression of ten emanations, proceeding from the summit to the base and returning back again to the summit. The two directions that the emanations progress represent the descending emanating waves of creation/involution and the ascending initiatory path of individual evolution/synergy. These ten emanations permeate the seven planes of consciousness of the individual, acting as a refracting prism to the creative processes of the Absolute Being. The revelation of this model is that it reveals the transformative powers of the individual acting as a miniature reflection of the creative powers of the Deity.

The ten emanations are refracted in each of the seven planes, thus making a total of seventy emanations that act as the powers of the fully actualized magician. We can imagine this simply as a vertical column of seven pyramids placed point to base. The ten emanations contained within each pyramid would be immersed in one of the seven planes. Thus the summit of the lower pyramid touches the base of the one on the next plane above, and these are arranged from the lowest plane to the highest, producing seventy emanations in all. This model is a macrocosmic model of the individual as the Deity, refracting through the seven planes of individual consciousness.

The pyramidal model of individual consciousness mirrors the Deity throughout its facets, being an image of the perfect form of that Deity, or what the Greek Philosophers called the Golden Ratio (Φ). This reveals the mystery behind the myth that humanity was created in the image of the Deity, or that in the image of humanity one may find the image of God.

Creative emanation is a process where the unified being of Deity expresses itself in ever-greater magnitudes of manifestation. Emanation of synergy is produced when sentient individuals unite and ultimately become one in emulation of the Absolute State of Being. Thus there is a spiritual expression of conscious-will that emanates from the Deity, and also from the individual. These contribute to the continual processes of involution (creation) and evolution (ascension). The two processes of creation and ascension represent the descending and ascending waves of emanation, the twin powers of creation and synergy. Emanation is the process of cause and effect within consciousness -- the magick of the individual and the co-creative powers of the Deity.

There are many models depicting the process of emanation, but this book uses the model defined by the Tree of Life as found in the Qabbalah. In this model, there are ten emanations called Sephiroth (Divine Numbers) representing the various stages at which the process of manifestation and evolution work.

The ten emanations suffuse the Seven planes of consciousness and are the powers by which these levels are defined and established. They begin with Mystery as the preexistent source, the paradoxical unmanifested Absolute State of Oneness, which generates the first manifestation as Union.

The first manifestation proceeds in turn to create nine other states of being that are characterized by the following words: Wisdom, Numen, Belief, Motive, Self (Identity), Values, Activity,

Image and Essence. These ten emanations represent the processes causing involution from the perfected unmanifested state of being known only as Mystery, to the ultimate but imperfect state of manifestation, known as Essence. These ten concepts are also directly analogous to the ten Sephiroth of the Tree of Life.

Following is a table that illustrates the ten emanations and how they interact with the seven planes of consciousness.

The Key of the 10 Emanations

Table of the 10 Emanations and the Seven Planes

Num	Qualities	7 Planes of Consciousness	Sephiroth of the Qabbalah	English Translation of Sephiroth
0	Mystery	Void	Ain Soph	Limitless Void
1	Union	Absolute	Kether	Crown
2	Wisdom	Spirit	Chokmah	Wisdom
3	Numen	Mind	Binah	Understanding
4	Belief	Higher Astral	Chesed	Mercy
5	Motive		Geburah	Strength
6	Self (Identity)		Tiphareth	Beauty
7	Values	Lower Astral	Netzach	Victory
8	Activity		Hod	Splendor
9	Image	Etheric	Yesod	Foundation
10	Essence	Physical	Malkuth	Kingdom

7.3.5 The Pentad - Five Categories of Symbolic Alignment

Having examined two models of consciousness based on the Ten Emanations and the Seven planes of consciousness, it is revealed that these models represent the powers of the Deity and the domain of human sentience, respectively. It has also been shown how these two models are integrated into a single structure illustrating the dynamic interplay of divine powers and human awareness; this is the Magick Pyramid.

In the *Disciple's Guide*, I revealed the six basic structures that make up the symbols of transformation. These six basic structures were the point, line, circle, triangle, cross and the star, which when allied with an altered state of consciousness, produces the phenomenon of ritual magick.[21] The symbols of transformation are incorporated into the actual body and structure of the ritual itself. They can also be used as ancillary symbols, as talismans and sigils, to imprint the magickal power that is raised in a ritual.

However, in regards to the specific ritual structures that are embedded into the magickal rituals employed by the magician, these six basic symbolic structures are not easily defined as ritual structures. In order to create an equivalency between ritual structures and symbols of transformations, I derived another model, combining them into a single set of categories.

This fourth model of consciousness assists the magician in understanding how to categorize and qualify ritual structures with regard to their effect on consciousness, or as symbols of transformation. I have named it Pentad because it consists of the five components which are the five distilled symbols of transformation in a ritual structure format.

The components of the Pentad are the five archetypes representing the relation and interaction between the magician and the Deity (as an occult ideal), and is the artifice of representing those relationships in the symbolic form of ritual patterns.

These symbolic forms are the attributes of the occult ideals used to give meaning to ritual structures, and they are called the Five Categories of Symbolic Alignment. These five categories also represent profound and exalted symbols of transformation as encountered in the performance of ritual magick in any magickal system.

The five categories could also be considered analogous to the five symmetrical solids of Pythagorean Philosophy, which supposedly embodied all physical substances. They were actually a method of symbolically categorizing the four Elements and Spirit in an immanent form, depicted as the basic crystalline structures of matter. They could also be seen as the mechanism of the ritual expression of symbols of conscious transformation.

The Pentad is also part of the integrated structure of the pyramidal model of consciousness (the Tetractys pattern: 4-3-2-1). The number five represents the pyramid as it is defined in three-dimensional space, with four points for the base and one for the apex. It represents the transcendent dimension beyond all space and

---

21   See *Disciple's Guide to Ritual Magick* by Frater Barrabbas – p. 42 - 43

time (the domain of Spirit), as contrasted to the four previous levels of the pyramid represented in only two dimensions.

The five categories of the Pentad symbolize the dynamic interplay of the ascending and descending emanating waves that cycle through the four levels of the pyramid.

In ritual magick, the five categories represent the essential dynamic and interactive structures of meaning and significance that tie all the elements of a ritual together, from the mind-state of magicians and the metaphysical beliefs that they espouse, to the tools that they wield and the magickal devices and profound declarations made within the sacred ritual space.

The five basic ritual structures are the keys that link the actions of magicians to the symbolic formulations of the Absolute. Whatever they release in their symbolic world has a corresponding analogue in the material and the archetypal worlds that is also released.

When we examine a ritual action and reduce it to its most abstract quality, what remains is the interplay between magicians acting as the divine mediator and the Deity representing the powers of creation and evolution. Because magicians have assumed the powers and authority of the Deity (through assumption), they have also assumed the powers of creation and evolution, and therefore every ritual action performed is an action precipitated by the Deity.

Therefore, when magicians perform a ritual action in a ritual, it has a profound symbolic effect and causes their conscious mind to undergo a subtle but potent transformation. As magicians perform a ritual action, they make a statement however implicit about the immediate relationship between themselves and the Deity. Therefore, ritual structures can only be understood in regards to the subtle but powerful effects that they cause in the soul and conscious mind of magicians, and the greater meaning that they impart from a spiritually symbolic perspective.

There are five basic ritual qualities that can be found from analyzing the rituals of a basic system of ritual magick, such as found in the *Disciple's Guide*. These qualities represent the most basic classifications of ritual meaning, and the various meta-symbols, ritual actions and expressions are grouped under one of them, representing that specific quality of spiritual relationship and interaction.

The five qualities are defined as a type of dynamic spiritual relationship that is expressed at the core of a ritual structure, known as the occult ideal. The magician may establish through a ritual structure an archetype qualified by a specific spiritual orientation, thus causing a corresponding magickal effect.

The five categories characterize the different spiritual relationships and magickal effects active in a basic system of ritual magick. If the magician understands these five categories and realizes their magickal effect, then any ritual can be analyzed and understood as to how it actually works. Magicians using this method can decipher that the magickal effect a ritual structure produces is due to the combination of one or more of these five qualities, and accordingly, they may endeavor to classify all of the ritual events in a ritual, and a ritual working. Therefore, the effect of a ritual can be understood even before the magician performs it.

The five categories of symbolic alignment represent the symbolic language of ritual and give meaning to the ritual actions and symbolic expressions that a magician performs. They are: Identity, Occurrence, Polarity, Alignment and Resonance.

Identity

IDENTITY

The first relationship is the statement of identity, the primordial Ehieh Asher Ehieh, "I will be whom I will be." When magicians symbolically express a declaration, then the quality of divine force that is channeling through them is altered. It becomes clarified and defined, and it exists as an ideal, as if for the first time before being summoned and made manifest from the Void. Whenever magicians name something, make a statement of intent or define their metaphysical beliefs in a ritual, the corresponding ritual action causes something on the symbolic plane to be created. Thus this relationship is one of creation and symbolizes the magician as Deity using its powers to further the divine process of creative emanation.

Occurrence

The second relationship represents a progression from one dimension (the "I am") to two dimensions (the "I am" and the "Thou"). The first relationship could be represented by the form of a single point in space, and the second relationship has produced a second point, thereby forming a line. The second relationship is defined as the state of differentiation--the condition in which the individual has realized the presence of another individual.

OCCURRENCE

When magicians draw lines of force with their magick dagger, erect a magickal pylon or perform divination, then the quality of occurrence is being used. Occurrence is the relationship of the self in contradistinction to others. Therefore, when magicians draw lines of force between two objects in the temple, they are said to be differentiated. It is in the same fashion that the Deity became aware of the need to differentiate itself, causing to be born the impetus to create. This relationship is the most paradoxical and it is aptly symbolized by the mirror, and the magician's Imago.

Polarity

The third relationship represents a further progression from one and two dimensions, producing a quality that is duality. Prior to this relationship, there was no consideration of the importance of others. There was only the tacit admittance that the individual was not alone and that the occurrence of the other was only a reflection of the self. Here, the self has realized the distinctness and separation of the other from itself. The other has become vested with significance and equal importance, and the self that believed that it was unique and infinite seeks to assimilate the other. The tension that the emergence of desire has produced is the basis for the power associated with polarity, and it represents the potential for union and further creation.

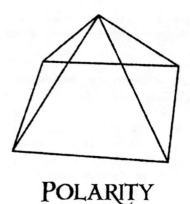

POLARITY

Therefore, all ritual actions that express the quality of polarity are able to generate fields of magickal power. Polarity is defined at its most basic level as the tension between the masculine and feminine states of being. The religious associations established between God and humanity has often been symbolized by human relationships. We are as different from the Deity as it is from us, but opposites attract and while we are drawn to this source of Unified Being, we also fear it. Magicians, however, have rejected the hypothesis that the Deity and humanity must be distinct and have therefore assumed the role of mediator, in which we act as the unbiased channel for the powers of the Deity.

Alignment

The fourth relationship represents the resolution of duality, thus producing union. It is the process of spiritual and material integration that represents the most important of magickal actions. The most obvious of these are the ritual actions of sacramentation and communion. Wherever matter is imbued with the quality of spirit, then a sacrament is produced.

For instance, the ritual action that purifies the area of the magick temple relies on the production of a sacrament, which is the lustral water. The salt and the water that make up the lustral water are independently charged, blessed and then mixed together. The salt represents the masculine polarity and the water represents the feminine, and joined together they fuse in

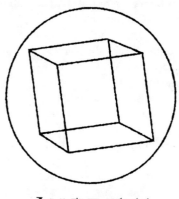

ALIGNMENT

union to produce a sacred substance. The quality of union represents a state of interconnection and interdependence, which defines the category of alignment.

Magicians are concerned with spiritual alignment because it controls the production of sacraments and assists them in establishing a transformative relationship of union with the Deity. These are the two most important functions in the practice of ritual magick. Magicians must assume not only the role but also the Spirit of the Deity into themselves in order to successfully perform these ritual actions. Without this relationship of union the symbolic ritual actions would be meaningless and the production of sacraments would be a fraudulent act. Magicians act through the authority and power of the Deity, producing the various phenomena of magick as the creative acts of the Godhead. What makes this possible is that there exists union between magician and Deity.

Resonance

The fifth and final relationship is represented by the climax of union, which is the state of ecstasy. If polarity generates magickal power, then ecstasy causes it to be exteriorized. The quality of ecstasy is produced in ritual magick through the process of resonance or intensification. Whenever a ritual action is intensified, the process of resonance is being used in that ritual so that its significance and impact will be greatly increased. It is through resonance that the processes of polarity and alignment are reduced to the simplistic state of identity. Through the power of ecstasy, all differences are nullified and all distinctions are melded into a single state of Being.

The word ecstasy comes from the Greek word ekstasis, which means out of the stillness. Thus ecstasy transports us beyond our current sphere of sensory perception and takes us to another world where the normal five senses are deemed irrelevant. Through the

RESONANCE

transformative process of ecstasy, we can ascend the levels of consciousness to become one with the consciousness of the Absolute Being. The level of resonance is determined by the level of intensity, with the magician controlling the intensity applied to the field of magickal power. Therefore, resonance is the key process that activates magickal power. It is also crucial to assisting magicians, through divine ecstasy, in the realization of themselves as the Deity.

These five categories are represented by five basic ritual structures each having many levels of expression. Yet throughout the different scales of representation, the basic quality of each ritual structure is essentially the same.

In addition, we will also compare these five basic ritual structures to the ten emanations of the Godhead, in order to further symbolically conceptualize them. In this fashion, the five categories will also have metaphysical and Qabbalistic definitions associated with them.

Five Categories as Ritual Structures

We have briefly covered the five categories as how they are metaphysically defined. Now we will examine them with regards to ritual structures so we can use them to decipher the effects of a ritual and a ritual working.

Ritual Structures of Identity

The ritualized statement of Identity is represented by the ritual structure known as the Midpoint. The Midpoint can be ritually represented as either the action of self-centering, establishing a center (as in the center of the magick circle) or the action of making a magickal statement or a definition. Therefore, all magickal statements function as a Midpoint. The Midpoint is also represented by the Star, principally the seven-sided star called the Septagram or Heptagram. The seven-sided star represents the definition of the Self as consisting of seven bodies functioning in the Seven planes of consciousness. For instance, the ritual action of defining an entity through the artifice of drawing the seven angles of the Septagram represents the action of self-definition through the magickal process known as Evocation.

The ritual structure of the Midpoint includes two processes of emanation that are symbolized by the numbers 1 and 7 on the Tree of Life. The numeral 1 symbolizes the process of Union and the numeral 7 symbolizes the process of Values. Therefore, the Midpoint represents the combined processes of emanation and qualification that define the holistic expression of the self, representing one's spiritual self-definition. The Midpoint is, of course, analogous to the symbol of transformation of the point.

Ritual Structures of Occurrence

The category of Occurrence is represented by the ritual structure of the Pylon, which is the physical joining of two opposite points, such as the two points in the center of the magick circle, the zenith and the nadir. If the magician joins these two points, a line of power is created between them. They are joined to establish a structure that acts as a channel (stairway or ladder) between what is symbolized as the Macrocosm and the Microcosm, contrasting the levels of the Deity and individual beings. The Pylon defines an entity in relationship to time and space as well as the nature of its spiritual essence. Therefore, this ritual structure defines the existence of an object.

The ritual structure of the Pylon includes one process of emanation symbolized by the number 2, which is Wisdom. However, there is an implicit symbolic quality to the Pylon that is symbolized by the unmanifested state of Mystery (the Limitless Void of the Tree of Life, symbolized by the zero).

These two emanations, Wisdom and Mystery, represent the quest for spiritual knowledge. This quest is defined as the discovery of a paradox, and the subsequent analysis and intuitive understanding of it (acceptance) that generates an integral knowledge. The quest for spiritual awareness represents the process by which the magician seeks to identify the ways of the World of the Spirit through the channel created by the Pylon. The end of the quest reveals the great hidden knowledge (Greater Arcana) that assists the magician in perfecting one's own magickal work. The author and the source of this hidden knowledge is the ultimate guide and teacher of the magician. The ritual structure of the Pylon is also analogous to the symbol of transformation of the line.

Ritual Structures of Polarity

The category of Polarity is symbolized by the magick Pyramid that includes the devices of the Rose Cross, Rose Ankh and the Pentagram. It is also symbolized by the ritual structure of a magick circle that is squared by the symbolic development of the Quarters or Angles, and where they are joined together within a central Pylon. The Pyramidal Pentagram ritual, found in the *Disciple's Guide* consists of this ritual structure, and represents the polarity of the archetypal masculine and feminine principals, and because of its linear structure it causes the generation of the masculine type of magickal power. This is because the energy pattern of the Pyramid is based upon a deosil circuit and a pyramidal shape.

The ritual structure of the Pyramid consists of two processes of emanation from the Tree of Life, which correspond to the symbolic numbers 5 and 10. These are the emanations of Motive and Essence. The emanation of Motive moves us to action. It is the principal motivator that gives power and strength to the quest for fulfillment. The emanation of Essence represents the potential for physical manifestation. Thus joined, they represent the polarity of ambition and manifestation that underlie all physical actions. The polarity between these two emanations represents the fundamental definition of magickal power, which is the internal tension created by desire. The Pyramid is analogous to the symbol of transformation of the cross, but has additional elements as well.

Ritual Structures of Alignment

The category of Alignment is represented by the Sphere (or Cube within a Sphere). This structure includes the devices of the Triangle (trigon), the Hexagram and the Enneagram (nine-pointed star), the ritual structures of the Gate, the generation of sacraments and the six positions of the magick circle as presented by the four Watchtowers, the Ultrapoint (zenith) and the Infrapoint (nadir).

The Sphere is essentially the structure of the magickal reality as defined in space and time, yet it transcends both. It is the world within a world, the domain of the intersection of the Macrocosm and the Microcosm, which is the Mesocosm. This ritual structure represents the process of mediation, and all ritual actions of mediation (especially any form of sacramental communion) are variations of it.

The ritual structure of the Sphere consists of three processes of emanation and these are symbolized by the numbers 3, 6 and 9. These three emanations are Numen, Self (Identity) and Image. The emanations of Self and Image represent the intellectual and unconscious expressions of the identity. When they are joined together, they become the synthesis of all conscious being. Therein the Numen is produced, which is the product of the joining of Self and Image. The addition of Numen causes the identity (both conscious and unconscious) to be connected to the Higher Self, thus generating a conduit for enlightenment. The spiritual relationship that is established is love (the desire for spiritual union). It is expressed through devotion and worship, even though it is a form of self worship (but only the Self as the God/dess Within). The Sphere is analogous to the symbol of transformation of the triangle, but could also include the circle.

Ritual Structures of Resonance

The category of Resonance is represented by the Spiral, the most sublime of the five ritual structures. The Spiral embodies the devices of the Equal Arm Cross, the Swastika and the ritual structure of the Octagram, which consists of the four Watchtowers in fusion with the four Angles. The Spiral also is represented as itself in the four different types of Spirals, as well as the ritual action of circumambulating the magick circle either deosil or widdershins.

The Spiral is a symbol of the vortex and it contains all the five basic ritual structures within itself. The vortex, as already stated, is the feminine quality of magickal power and represents the base for all complex magickal workings. The vortex contains and maintains all that is performed within it and projects waves of emanations of magickal power at harmonic intervals of time and intensity.

The vortex is the superior method of manifesting changes to occur in physical reality, and causing those changes to become manifest and permanently established. The vortex represents a type of power that is not direct but potently magnetic and invocative, and therefore more efficacious than the independent use of the masculine quality of power. When a magician performs a ritual that generates the masculine quality of magickal power within a vortex, then the resultant super-polarity represents the ultimate maximization of magickal power and intensifies the results of the magickal working.

The ritual structure of the Spiral consists of two emanations that are symbolized by the numbers 4 and 8. The symbolic quality of 4 is that of Beliefs (the basic concepts that make up the occult world view), which is the foundation for all further manifestation. In order to interact with the world, one must first have some basic assumptions about its nature. These assumptions are always established through faith because they cannot be proven objectively. Our base of beliefs allows us to be capable of activity, therefore, the numeral 4 leads irresistibly to the numeral 8 (the emanation of Action).

Once a body of beliefs has been established, then the magician may proceed with an action in complete confidence of its success. An action committed without confidence is both weak and irrelevant, whereas a confident action has the power of the Deity behind it. While belief is the foundation of the magician's power, it is the power of action precipitating movement that generates and releases magickal power. The combination of faith and action causes the generation of meaning and the experience of the activated power of magick. The Spiral is analogous to the symbol of transformation of the circle, the cross, and also has additional qualities as well.

Using the Five Categories of Ritual Structures

The combination of the processes of emanation and spiritual relationship produce the five basic categories expressed in the basic ritual structures. Yet each of these ritual structures consist of various devices and ritual structures in themselves, establishing a repertoire of various magickal representations and expressions for the generation of specific functional magickal effects.

The five fundamental ritual structures always adhere to the basic requirements of a ritual. It must consist of three parts and establish an emphasis or a climax if it is the last ritual structure in a given working.

The five categories of ritual action and spiritual alignment are qualities that impact the performance of ritual structures. The sequence of the actions and their significance represent the core processes that are active in a ritual. A simple ritual pattern will use all of the above categories to generate magickal power, imprint it with symbolic meaning and exteriorize it so that it may fulfill its set objective.

However, a more complex working requires a series of rituals, each performing a specific function. These are connected together through the use of a synopsis. Rituals that have a specific function are used in combinations, so they need not recapitulate all the forms that a simple ritual requires. By emphasizing a specific category or quality, these rituals are able to embody their associated function and express it as a stage in the overall ritual process of the working.

A modular system of magick uses rituals that exclusively express a specific function. Functional rituals are used to build up rituals workings, and can be reused for other ritual workings. There are specific patterns that can be followed to formulate certain kinds of workings, but in each ritual working, the intent of the magician is unique.

This approach was used in the formulation of the advanced rituals used in the E.S.S.G., and even adapted in the grimoire of the *Disciple's Guide*. It represents a milestone in the advancement of the practice of ritual magick, since it becomes easy to formulate a ritual working and then perform it.

There are seven basic functional rituals needed to compose the ritual workings of an intermediate practice of ritual magick. These seven functions consist of the rituals of Consecration, Empowerment, Passage (the Gate), Alignment and the cyclic Mysteries: the mysteries of the Moon, the mysteries of the Sun, and the mysteries of the Initiation. These seven functions are loosely represented in the grimoire of the *Disciple's Guide*, and are a hallmark of the rituals of the E.S.S.G.

Thus five ritual structures are used to create the rituals that satisfy the seven basic functional needs of a ritual magician. The discipline inherent in the proper use of these functions enables the ritual to become an effective instrument for self-determination and spiritual enlightenment.

Magicians first seek through these rituals to establish their identity, then to fulfill their basic needs and desires, thereby fortifying one's place in life. Magicians then undertake the quest for self-realization using the dual processes of self-transformation and spiritual union to realize spiritual illumination and enlightenment. Whatever direction this quest takes, it ultimately reveals to magicians the nature of their destiny - to be an agent of the Deity. Therefore, magicians proceed from the primary initiatory degree symbolized by the element Earth. This first initiatory degree consists of the development of the self and evolves to the exalted degree of avatarship wherein magicians commit to the selfless act of spiritual service for the world at large.

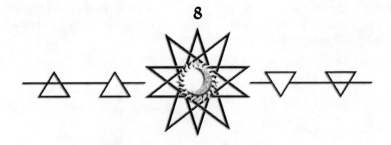

Performance of Ritual

8.1 Introduction

Ritual performance concerns itself with choreography and theatrical blocking, i.e., the movements, dialogue and expression of ritual as performed in sacred space. This section reveals the basic components of the actual performance of ritual, which is the assembling of the basic ritual structures to form the specific types of magickal rituals. The basic types of magickal rituals are the seven functional groups mentioned previously. This section is also divided into two parts. The first will outline the performance components of ritual (the choreography and theatrical blocking) and the second will give an explanation of the pattern of the basic ritual workings.

We must concern ourselves first with the expressions of magickal power as they are used in rituals, the techniques of ritual movement (ritual action) and the ritual processes that generate magickal power through resonance.

The magickal expression of power consists of the intoned words of power and the ritual actions that express magickal power as the inspiration caused by the resonance of ecstasy. In either state, the mind and the emotions are greatly inspired and thereby profoundly transformed.

Rituals that express magickal power consist of two action components. There is the drawing of symbolic devices and the performance of repetitive ritual actions done through resonance. All this is performed by a magician who has adopted the appropriate mind-state beforehand.

Every action and utterance that is significant to the magician, performed in sacred space, produces effects deemed magickal.

Symbols and myths are given life through the magician's philosophies and expressions, conveying individual meaning through a representation of archetypal significance.

The performance of ritual magick is essentially spiritual theater. The circle acts as stage. The tools are props. The combination of movement, speech and emotion comprise the script. The audience is the Deity, and the impact of the performance is received through the medium of the World of the Spirit in conjunction with the mundane world.

Just as in the mundane world the myths and tales expressed in a community theater performance has an effect and impact on the community, spiritual theater through ritual magick effects and impacts the consciousness of the magician, and ultimately the world at large.

8.2 Magickal Expressions of Power

Expressions of magickal power in various Grimoire include, but are certainly not limited to, the utterance of statements, the chanting of words or phrases (such as mantras), circumnambulating a magick circle, drawing magickal symbols, devices, lines of force or engaging in ecstatic dance

All magickal actions are linked together and performed as dance, giving ritual performance its flowing patterns, dynamic interactions and artistic expressions. Practice of the techniques allows mastery to create an aesthetic and graceful expression of the performance of ritual magick.

A great ritual magician is known by the perfected drama and the flowing choreography presented in the ritual performance. Good ritual is dependent upon confident movement and execution that only practice and familiarity can provide.

8.3 Magickal Words of Power

Choreography and statements of personal spiritual significance stimulate the body and the mind simultaneously. Statements, or words of power, comprise the narrative part of the ritual, weaving the symbolic correspondences into a fabric of purpose and intention.

Narration reveals why the ritual is being performed, the nature of its symbolic components and their combined essential meaning. Orisons and exhortations are offered to the Deity, thus defining and animating it. There are also specific words of power that act as acronyms, representing a formulation of specific correspondences.

Nothing stands alone in a ritual. All statements and actions are an artifice representing the true and unnamed essential archetypes found in the collective unconscious. All magickal symbols represent analogous qualities at a deep level of reality. That depth is inexplicable to the individual conscious mind because its origins are in the domain of Spirit. Yet these symbols act as a mediator between the inexplicable and the known, unlocking the latent power of their potential so that they may be known by their effect. Therefore, symbols, images, concepts, arcane names, and barbarous words of evocation (verba ignota) represent the intellectual and conceptual expressions found in ritual.

There are two methods for verbal expressions in ritual magick. The first method is conceptual and intellectual. The second is formulaic cyclic chanting of mantras. In cyclic chanting, words are used to cause resonance through emphasis, repetition and accelerated articulation. Words spoken in this manner are almost sung, giving them a musical quality called intoning. Therefore, mantras or magickal formula words are intoned so that the voice has an eerie ringing bell-like quality. When a magician chants a phrase in this sonorous manner, it causes the magickal atmosphere of the temple or grove to resonate, increasing the tension and elevating the level of power that the magician experiences. A repetitive chant serves as a kind of generator of energy and the movement of words acts as a surrogate for bodily movement, and it can be used to raise magickal energy and project it outward. Intoning a phrase causes the meaning and significance of the words themselves to be emphasized and empowered. These empowered words and phrases impact the unconscious mind of the magician and charge the atmosphere of the ritual working.

A magician can perform a ritual without verbal expressions, totally relying on the ritual actions and the ritual pattern to silently impart all the necessary meaning and power. Conversely, the magician can perform a ritual using only the verbal expressions, producing magickal effects by the power of words alone. The underlying process of ritual magick is a form of symbolic communication that consists of both verbal expressions and actions. As a phenomenon of language, ritual magick can rely on both forms (words and actions), or use just one of them to effectively communicate the meaning of the ritual.

The communication process of ritual can be understood as occurring simultaneously between magicians, their psyche, the collective unconscious mind of humanity and the superconscious being of the Deity. The direction of communication is always two-way. The symbolic communication of ritual magick as performed by magicians is received by the collective mind, interpreted, and then reflected back in a subtle but potent contact that utterly transforms them, and by extension, the world at large.

The combination of words of power and ritual actions represents the most potent and effective form of ritual performance. The words of power are thus integrated with the expressions and actions of ritual. This forges a ritual working with the maximum potential for transformation, uniting both symbols of transformation and heightened states of consciousness.

8.4 Circumambulations

As previously stated, the magick circle is the boundary of magickal activity where the defined focus represents the symbolized macrocosm superimposed upon the microcosm of the magician.

The energy flow of the magick circle is around its circumference and is bi-directional. Use of polarity of the center and the periphery of the circle allows for the occurrence of a spiral that circles both inward and outward, representing the two directions of the power of magick (involution and evolution; liberation and manifestation). The magician emulates these processes by walking with grace and deliberation along the perimeter of the magick circle, defining the flow of magickal power within its two dimensions. The ritual movement is translated directly as magickal power and the act of circumambulating the magick circle either deosil or widdershins is a method of expressing that magickal power.

A circumambulation begins and ends at the same place, thus making a complete circuit. Where the ritual action begins and ends (positions of the circle) is as significant as the direction in which one proceeds. The classic circumambulation pattern is modeled after the passage of the Sun that rises in the East and proceeds in a deosil circuit to the West, where it proceeds around the other side of the planetary sphere until it reaches the East once again. This circuit begins in the Eastern Ward of the circle (represented by the Element of Air) and passes the final position as the Northern Ward (represented by the Element of Earth). This circuit begins with the Element of Air (Ideals) and ends with Earth (Matter) before returning again to Air, thus representing the circuit of manifestation.

Similarly, the circuit that begins in the Northern Ward and proceeds widdershins, passing the final position as the Eastern Ward, represents the generation of the power of liberation. The transition from Earth (Matter) to Air (Ideals) is the opposite of the circuit of manifestation, and represents the evolution of matter into spirit and the liberation of the mind.

The deosil circuit causes magickal power to be focused, and therefore intensified. The widdershins circuit causes magickal power to be released and exteriorized. Much of the movement of ritual consists of circumambulating the arc of the magick circle or forming a spiral by the magician walking out those patterns. Spirals integrate the components of the four Wards and Angles so that a unified expression is formed and drawn together, where it is realized in the center of the circle. Circumambulations can join circle components, or cause them to be polarized, depending on the direction.

The magician walks solemnly and with great deliberation, performing at each Angle or Ward whatever additional actions are required to express their qualities. The movement is graceful, determined, flowing and liberating. The significance of the direction is not omitted, because part of the magician's deliberation consists of the knowledge and familiarity with the quality of each position and expressing it the moment one passes it. The magician's breathing is slow and steady, mixed in with moments of cool breathing, expressing the magickal power that is being generated.

8.5 Drawing Lines of Force

In addition to circumambulating the magick circle and drawing spiral patterns to assist the flow of magickal energy, the magician may draw lines of force between objects, draw symbolic devices in the air or etch them on the ground. The magician may also trace the lines of an illustrated talisman in order to activate it. Tools such as the wand, dagger, staff, or sword assist the artifice of drawing of lines of force, giving the process a special emphasis as qualified by that tool.

For instance, drawing lines of force with an athamé represents a very masculine kind of energy (a cutting, dividing or etching) that symbolizes the particular attributes associated with Air, which is thought and action. The use of the naked hand to draw the lines of force represents that the act itself is significant. The naked hand is the tool of utmost sincerity, representing the purity of focus and action when used alone.

The athamé or magick dagger has very specific ritual uses and is limited by its aggressive qualities. An athamé would never be used to invoke a spirit or a God, and in fact would never be used to attract a being at all. The athamé, and to greater extent the sword, is a weapon as well as a tool, protecting the wielder and directing the flow of magickal energies. The athamé is used to draw invoking or banishing pentagrams and to charge certain sacraments (such as the lustral water) by acting as the mediator of the masculine polarity of magickal power. The abilities to divide and direct lines of energy and demarcate boundaries are the principal uses of the dagger and the sword.

The wand is used to invoke, attract, and draw objects together to unite them. Because of its symbolic association with the phallus, it represents the masculine magickal energies in a softer and more intimate fashion than the athamé. The naked erect penis represents that state of extreme vulnerability and trust associated with positive and ideal expressions of sexual love; for as a fleshy organ, it is vulnerable to any kind of violence. There is an implied feminine perspective in the masculine expression of the power of the wand, and it is used to summon spirits and God/desses by being waved in the air, drawing invoking spirals. The wand is used to draw the four types of spirals when they are used without other symbolic devices; thus the wand performs the ritual actions of invoking, banishing, sealing and unsealing.

When a crystal is secured to its tip, the wand becomes a tool that can be used as both a wand and a dagger, also called a transmutar wand. It is commonly utilized in higher forms of ritual magick.

The staff, as a large wand, is used as a support for the magician and as a symbol of authority. Some magicians believe that a staff is more powerful than a sword. It is rarely used to draw lines of force, but can be positioned horizontally over the magician's head, held by both hands and then carefully turned as the magician turns in place. The staff is used in specific body postures that can represent certain states of being, such as receptivity, reflection, authority and projection. The staff adds a great emphasis when held in either the front of the magician or at ones side. The image of a magician holding a staff while intoning incantations or exhortations projects an image of authority. The staff is the perfect magickal symbol of spiritual authority, the rule of wisdom as opposed to the rule of force, as expressed by the sword.

8.6 Ecstatic Dance Techniques

The ritual action of circumambulation has certain logistical limitations associated with the number of participants. This ritual action is easiest performed by one individual.

When more participants are involved, circumambulation becomes a choreographed operation of ritual dance. Choreography is important for the sake of the smooth and uninterrupted expression of the movement, and the coordination of that movement for more than one person. This does not prohibit the solitary practitioner from dancing alone, but it is quite difficult for more than a few people to circumambulate together.

Where circumambulation has the function of uniting or polarizing the constituents of the magick circle, ritual dance causes the energy to powerfully resonate, greatly increasing its intensity and quickly exteriorizing it.

The action of uniting or polarizing a magick circle is easily done by one individual, but ritual dance requires the necessary organizing and synchronization of group movement. This type of ritual dance uses resonance, where the dancing increases in tempo and intensity, and it is completed with some form of climax that is typified as a sudden change of direction, a sudden cessation of movement, or an explosive outburst of breath and voice.

This simplest example of ritual dance imitates the children's game "Ring Around the Rosy", in which the children hold hands and then walk, skip or run in a circle together. The movement is repeated and speed increased along with the tempo of the song until a climax of activity is reached, and the participants suddenly "all fall down" to their hands and knees. The associated chant, although quite childlike, disguises a more serious and ancient purpose of raising magickal power to ward off the plague, and this childish game is therefore actually the vestige of an old ritual.

This pattern has already been discussed in regard to the witches' circle dance and the raising and exteriorizing of a cone of power. It is performed as a joyous outburst of desire and ecstasy, in which the participants give themselves wholly to the experience of their physical bodies while in a highly altered state of consciousness. When they reach the end of their physical endurance, they produce one final united verbal expression and a burst of exerted effort before falling to the earth in a swoon, pretended or real.

The ultimate dance is the dance of desire and resistance that is seduction. This is the dance of life and death that occurs between contending partners as expressed by the polarities of the archetypal male and female. The courtship dances of tribal men and women have a profoundly spiritual and religious value that is only dimly perceived in the youthful antics of Western rock and roll. Ritual dance has a magickal quality due to the transformative powers of ecstasy that it produces in the dancers. Those who attend rave gatherings are modern participants of this magickal process. It has also subtly pervaded our culture for hundreds of years disguised as the joy of public dancing, and it probably will continue to be an ongoing phenomenon for untold generations to come.

The performance of ecstatic dance represents the process of emotional and physical bonding, intensified through extreme stimulation and through repetitive and spontaneous physical movements. There is a cyclic or iterative quality to the body movements, causing a flowing return of feelings and sensations that disrupts linear reasoning. The resonance of the dance occurs when the frequency of the actions are incrementally increased until a climax is reached, followed by a period of cessation and stasis.

The symbolic quality of this dance technique is that of the union of heaven and earth as spirit and matter, wherein the very definition of human existence is expressed. The culmination of the effects of this dance is the union of both psychic and physical polarities and the momentary bliss it produces. That moment of bliss is the lure and the reward for those who participate in it. The potent attraction of dance is a social power that continues to haunt our world and imbue it with magick and wonder.

When a couple works a magickal ritual together, the dynamic quality of their polarized energies can be used in ecstatic dance to raise their feelings to a higher level, intensifying them until a psychic fusion draws them physically together. This psychic fusion is the cause of the feelings of bliss. The resonance experienced first suffuses the magick circle with an energy field, then ultimately causes it to be exteriorized. The sex act itself may be ritually dramatized, thus causing a powerful emanation of magickal power, and it is qualified by the sentiment and significance of the joining.

The process of ritualized sex requires the highest level of intimacy and sensitivity from those who engage in it as a magickal action. There are stringent requirements for the practice of sex magick, as such an act should not be taken lightly. Ritual sex is sacramental sexuality and is engaged by two physical beings who are as the God and Goddess. Sexual magick, when correctly performed, produces a psychic cataclysm that causes the direct manifestation of the powers of the Absolute Spirit. In the ensuing personal illumination, the couple experiences the fusion of the archetypal male and female, the Union of Being and the bliss of eternal ecstasy. However, to achieve this sublime height, the couple must alter the nature of their relationship from that of a common conjugality to a spiritually based hierosgamos. The petty ego must be extinguished and replaced by the inspiration of the Divine Will. Also, the couple must maintain during the period of sacramental workings a relationship that is both dynamic and peaceful. Few indeed are able to sacrifice their egos in order to produce the basis for a perfect and spiritual relationship. Thus a couple correctly practicing sexual magick must seem to emulate the glory of the Deity within their ardent embrace.

The rigors of sexual magick are very demanding and couples must engage in a long period of preparation before integrating it into their magickal practice. Those who are involved in such a working should be experienced with their own sexuality and comfortable in expressing it. It is perhaps unnecessary to point out that brief encounters between strangers can't produce the level of significance and spiritual identification that two experienced partners can generate. Therefore, sexual magick is not a kick nor is it performed for some cheap thrill; it is a profoundly moving experience expressing the qualities of love and physical union at their highest spiritual level.

9

Initiation: Cycle of Revelations

The most important process that ritual magicians undergo is transformative initiation. Whatever else they may pursue in their long and (hopefully) productive careers, the achievement of enlightenment is uttermost. And enlightenment is only achieved through the continual exposure to transformative initiation. True initiation occurs only through profound transformations. It can't be forced by the one undergoing it, nor can it be awarded by others. Transformation is a cyclic process, and each time magicians undergo it, they achieve a certain degree of growth, insight, and even wisdom. Over time, these continual transformations herald and precipitate major changes in the life and the mind of the magician.

Transformation even affects the soul, opening the magician to a greater overall awareness of one's self, and one's perspective of Deity. Transformative initiation is where the magician activates, however briefly, the God/dess Within, and merges mundane reality with that of the World of Spirit, and the Godhead that lives within it.

Many magickal organizations boast of being able to judge and award their initiates initiatory degrees that supposedly confer upon the candidate a higher and elevated state of being. However, most fail in being able to deliver on that boast, since what is being judged and measured is actually inexplicable, and no one can either demand or award a truly life-changing transformation. It is something that happens, but typically (though not always) it happens to those who ardently seek it. Devoted sages who love their Deity, and who seek it both within and without themselves, will ultimately find what they seek out. Spiritual yearning is often rewarded, but seldom immediately, and usually not until after a long period of contemplation, devotion and spiritual service.

Ritual Magicians seek to advance their knowledge of magick and the World of the Spirit, and as such, they inadvertently discover the key to their own enlightenment. This key is found in the knowledge of the cycle of transformative initiation. Magicians who grasp this key learn to build ritual mechanisms that cause transformations to deliberately occur, and so they are more readily able to wisely seek their path and find fulfillment, both spiritually and materially; for within the tradition of magick, the two different realities are actually one and the same.

The most astonishing realization about transformative initiation is that it's a process well known to all humanity. We see it endlessly depicted in books, movies, cable programs and even video games. Wherever there is a hero or heroine undergoing a great adventure, consisting of trials, incredible challenges and feats, near death escapes, and finally, deliverance and restoration we find the pattern of transformative initiation. We even see this pattern in biblical stories, and in the life, death and resurrection of the Christ. In all cultures and in all times of human history, this cycle of the hero or heroine has been depicted in some form and celebrated as the greatest story ever told. Taken in its ultimate form, it is the story of how a man or woman undergoes transformation and becomes a god or goddess.

We are immersed in this cycle of the hero or heroine, since it is the story of the transformation of a mortal human. This is a story that appeals to all humanity, for it even hints at immortality and godlike powers. The promise of immortality and godlike powers is intoxicating, and often when faced with a difficult life, or worse, one that is stultifying and boring, it can represent a kind of escape. Often, this story of a human being becoming a god is devalued as mere fiction, but then it lingers on in our spiritual teachings and our religion. If we could but dare, perhaps we could be like the great sage who founded his own religion and achieved immortality.

However, magicians realize that this cycle of initiation and transformation is a symbolic analogy of spiritual and psychological processes that exist in all human beings. While some fantasize and others feel themselves unworthy, magicians seek to penetrate the mystery, and unleash the spiritual process of continual transformation within themselves. Perhaps it's impossible to obtain immortality or become like a god, but it's not impossible to obtain enlightenment or complete mastery of one's self, or to gain a state of at-one-ment with the Deity; this is the ultimate goal of transcendental magick.

We must understand this cycle of initiation and learn to transformation ourselves so we might master our own spiritual path and obtain that which we seek, whether or not we are even aware of what that goal really is. Perhaps we are even heartened by our lack of insight, proceeding blindly, for it is said that even fools obtain enlightenment eventually. And that is how the hero always begins his quest, as the innocent and unknowing fool.

9.1 Introduction

The cycle of Transformative Initiation is the archetypal pattern of human spiritual evolution. This pattern consists of twenty-two stages within four realms, depicting the passage of the initiate into and out of the domain of the collective unconscious, called the Underworld. Once entry is gained, the initiate undergoes a supreme transformative ordeal, and then returns to the world of the light, bearing a renewed vision of the self and its place in the world. The cyclic nature of this pattern is continually repeated in the magickal progress of the magician, giving a spiral nature to the process of spiritual evolution.

Of all places, I discovered the pattern of transformative initiation in the writings of Joseph Campbell, particularly in the book, *The Hero with a Thousand Faces*. I found that the number of stages that the hero undergoes in Campbell's book was exactly twenty-two! As a magician and occultist, the number twenty-two is quite significant, since it's the number of letters in the Hebrew alphabet and the number of trumps in the Tarot. I was astonished, and eagerly began comparing the stages of the cycle of the hero with the trumps of the Major Arcana of the Tarot to see if there were any other similarities besides sharing the number twenty-two, and much to my amazement, they matched perfectly.

The reasoning that led Campbell to choose exactly twenty-two stages is unknown, and therefore it was probably an arbitrary deduction on his part. However, when I discovered that the twenty-two stages in the literary examples of the mythic hero's journey matched the twenty-two trumps of the Major Arcana of the Tarot, I also found a great key to understanding the pattern of initiation. It is a truism that a magician seldom believes in coincidences, especially when the results are so meaningful. Therefore, the original initiation cycle was deliberately hidden in myth, literature and in the trump cards of the Tarot. What were undefined and hidden were the actual detailed stages of this pattern, which Joseph Campbell revealed and made abundantly clear.

In The Hero with a Thousand Faces, Campbell gives a detailed explanation of each of the twenty-two stages in the Hero's Journey. They are divided into four sections, representing major distinctive features of this cyclic process.

* Section 1 – Descent, wherein the hero gains entry to the Underworld or faraway land and experiences a transformative change.
* Section 2 - The Ordeal (the Supreme Ordeal), as the process whereby the hero was united with his shadow half, and through this integration received in the form of a vision a renewed basis for life, called the magickal boon.
* Section 3 - The Revelation of the Vision, the Cosmic Cycle, which was the basis for the magickal boon.
* Section 4 - The Return, where the hero and his vision (boon) were reintegrated into the world of humanity.

The twenty-two stages of the cycle of the hero can now be compared to the Trumps of the Tarot. However, the sequence of Roman numerals at the heading of the Trumps (except the Fool) appear to represent the arrangement of the cards as they compare to the Paths on the Tree of Life in the Qabbalah, with the Fool being first and assigned the numeral zero. But the arrangement of the cards for the Cycle of Initiation is based upon the mythic journey of the hero. The resultant pattern is logical only in terms of the sequence of events of the hero's journey.

The following paragraphs will define in detail the twenty-two stages of the cycle of initiation, and also the Trumps (Atus) of the Tarot that match each stage.[22] In these stages the hero or seeker is considered a male. There is also a separate cycle for a woman or heroine, and this is discussed in section 9.3.3.

---

[22] The names of the Tarot Trumps are taken from the Crowley-Harris Thoth Tarot deck.

9.2 The Twenty-Two Stages of the Cycle of Initiation

TWENTY-TWO STAGES
OF THE
CYCLE OF INITIATION
*
SEAL OF SOLOMON

Part I - The Separation or Departure[23]

1. The Summoning or Call to Adventure; the Revelation of the Vocation of the Hero (Atu: XX - The Last Judgment)

As a proclamation that the process of self-transformation is about to commence, the initiate receives a warning from the mythical herald that announces the coming crisis. The call occurs not when our lives are comfortably sheltered, but only when we come to the precipice of our psychic existence. This occurrence of warning or the heralding of drastic changes can be seen in the unfolding of world history, and as an analogy, the call is not always perceived as such both by the individual facing a personal crisis and by the world. However, if the call is heeded then it begins a process of self-awakening that represents the first step in the transformation of the self. The crisis has occurred because the present institutions and societal solutions are no longer effective. In the individual, this represents that stage of life where the old methods of living and coping have become outmoded and the identity of the self is dangerously unsupported.

2. The Refusal of the Call; Folly or Internalization (Atu: 0 - The Fool)

The call has its opposite in the powers of inertia and resistance to change. Often this problem of inertia can only delay the inevitable changes, and can make them more difficult, even negative. The powers of inertia preserve the fabric of the social structure and bolster the identity of the individual with contrived defense mechanisms. However, these forces also slow down the initiative of even resourceful individuals and insulates them from new ideas and information. But the resistance to change is ultimately futile and they come whether or not the individual or the world is prepared.

The obstinate refusal of the call has its effects in the loss of personal direction and control, thus causing one to be at the mercy of capricious elements. The result of this loss of control may represent the disintegration of all order both in the self and in the world. However, the loss of control may instead indicate a willed introversion that represents the need of the individual to digest the purpose of the changes and then to submit to them under one's own

---

[23]   See *Hero with a Thousand Faces* by Joseph Campbell – p. 49 - 95

terms. The seeker who has received the call may need a pause in the action of life to integrate the new forces emerging in the wake of change and realize the overall significance of the event.

3. Supernatural Aid or Intervention; Meeting the Spirit Guide (Atu: II - The Priestess)

When change finally does occur it is experienced as a supernatural event that is all-encompassing and also predetermined. Herein the hero encounters the Guide of the Pathways, the teacher or elder who will direct the seeker through the ordeals of self-transformation by offering hope as a protective force. The Guide offers to the hero a glimpse of what is to be gained if the ordeal can be mastered, which is that state of perfection that was known at the beginning of life, the singular, "I AM." The domain associated with the Guide is the sanctuary, the temple as refuge and place of spiritual teaching. The Guide often manifests in society as leaders of great tenacity and resourcefulness who appear in times of trouble to assist humanity through a crisis.

4. Crossing the First Threshold; Meeting the Fierce Guardian (Atu: IX - The Hermit)

After the Guide has been met, the seeker encounters the Guardian who stands before the threshold of the underworld that presages the dark night of the soul. The threshold represents the limit of what is permitted by society or is capable of definition by the self. The Guardian is the principal obstruction or issue that has caused the transformative powers to be unleashed. The seeker must resolve this issue and receive its wisdom in order to freely pass. In the act of crossing the threshold this limit has been irreparably penetrated and the consequences are represented by the fact that there can be no turning back. Beyond the boundaries of the known are the limitless possibilities of the unknown. Therein the conscious identity faces the prospect of being absorbed into the world of the shadow (our negative self-image) and the magick of the collective unconscious.

5. The Belly of the Whale; the Underworld (Atu: XVI - The Blasted Tower)

Once the threshold is crossed and the Guardian overcome, the seeker enters the world of the collective unconscious, which is the domain of the inner mind, the soul of humanity. The underworld is like a subterranean temple or grotto wherein the mysteries of the soul are revealed. The structure of the old self is completely destroyed and the seeker is forced to reintegrate the self along new parameters. This begins the process of the transformation of the self, for the old outmoded ways have been invalidated and the new way has yet to be defined.

Part II - The Trials and Victories of Initiation[24]

1. The Road of Trials; the Dangers and Lesser Ordeals (Atu: X - The Wheel of Fortune)

After the seeker has crossed the threshold and undergone the death of the old self, the fragmented facets that remain are forced into awareness so that the seeker may succeed in overcoming the lesser ordeal of the trials of life and death. These trials cause the melding of the seeker's purpose and the elimination of all the irrelevant ideals and beliefs that were part of the fragmented facets of the old self. This is a process of purification through attrition and negation, but also definitive of what is newly relevant and significant.

2. Meeting the Goddess; Infancy Regained (Atu VI - The Lovers)

The ultimate ordeal is represented as the marriage of Light and Darkness, the reunification of the self. This can be perceived as a peaceful joining, the result of the successful completion of the trials. It can also be represented as the choice between alternate possibilities, or as the conflict of good and evil, Light and Darkness. The world has been reduced to a mythic polarity that requires either a peaceful integration, the domination of one force by the other or a complete annihilation, which is the reduction of the self to its core.

The dominant theme in this stage consists of the revelation of the powers of the Goddess, the feminine archetype. These powers are the dual forces of life, death and their associated metamorphosis in the World of the Spirit and the world of the flesh. The womb of the feminine archetype is also the tomb, making the regenerative process beyond all evaluations of good and evil despite the fact that it manifests as both Light and Darkness. The Goddess is also the Queen of the Mysteries because of her association with the cycles of

---

[24]   See *Hero with a Thousand Faces* by Joseph Campbell – p.97 - 192

the Moon and the rebirth of nature in the Spring. Therefore, she is also the agent of the transformative powers both in physical nature and the human psyche. Thus the powers of magick are both within and without the self.

3. Woman as Temptress; Agony of Separation (Atu XI - Strength)

This particular stage has two distinct definitions associated with it: The first represents the perspective that is part of the old age of Pisces -- the joining of the Light and Darkness in the prior stage must not imbalance the seeker and cause seeking of the Darkness over the Light. It also represents the fact that self-indulgence must be avoided in order to purify the self; therefore, it is also the path of asceticism.

The second definition is nearly the opposite: Through the passions evoked by the stimulation of the senses and the resultant ecstasy that they cause, the seeker is delivered to the transcendent level of existence. This is done not by the denial of human nature, but by its affirmation and exaltation.

These two definitions are like the opposite sides of the same coin in that they both represent the same thing. The most basic and common spiritual issue is found in both the renunciation of the world and the renunciation of limitation and denial. Both definitions represent a divergence from the blind acceptance of societal values. The world as it has been conceived is therefore rejected.

4. Atonement with the Father; Establishment of Inner Values (Atu: XV - The Devil)

Once the seeker has abandoned the normally accepted social values and renounced self-limitation and denial, then the seeker must abandon the old personal identity itself, with all its associated habits and superstitions. Therefore, the seeker experiences the lifting of the guilt of self-judgment and reestablishes a connection with the Deity that is more relevant to the true nature of the inner self than what was previously held. Abandoning of the old self-image is very difficult because we are bound to our petty ego by ingrained habits and self-sustaining defense mechanisms. To undergo this process of severing, we must seemingly die a second time since crossing the Underworld threshold. The subsequent rebirth of a spiritual identity represents atonement for harboring the false identity that had erected a barrier between the self and the Absolute.

This stage also represents the traditional idea of an initiation. After the candidate has been stripped of all egocentric support and purged of all inferior motivations and pursuits, one is invested with the vocation and responsibility of being a proper mediator for the Absolute Spirit. Thus he becomes the agent for forces that are beyond the domain of the narrow perspective of individuals, and these concerns the societal and cosmic levels of being. The initiate has received a role in the divine plan and a vocation as a reward for having passed the tests of initiation. Thus the initiate has taken a great step towards becoming the initiator and dispenser of a spiritual lineage and has assumed the earthly role of that of the All-Father, filled with the peace and serenity associated with the replacement of blind faith with knowledge and the certainty of experience.

5. Apotheosis; Self as Exalted Being (Atu: I - The Magician)

The initiate has now reached the core of the underworld, having bravely passed all tests and assumed all transformations. Thus, oneness is achieved with the highest spiritual expression of the self and has passed beyond the veil of bondage to the petty vicissitudes of life. The initiate is now truly liberated, and the values of good and evil are no longer meaningful. Because the self is no longer encumbered by the cares of life and reunited with its eternal spiritual double (the Higher Self, or God Within), the seeker is wrapped in the mantle of glory and exaltation of spiritual truth. The seeker is also prepared to share in the greater mystery of the Cosmic Cycle, for the barriers between the Absolute and the individual have been removed with the destruction of the petty ego and there is nothing that stands in the way of the pure vista of the Absolute Spirit and its evolving and emanating processes.

6. The Ultimate Boon; the secret knowledge of the soul is revealed. (Atu: VII - The Chariot)

From the Absolute Spirit the initiate receives a vision that consists of the secret knowledge of the seeker's soul, which is one's individual place within the divine plan. This potent affirmation causes the part of life that it touches to become inviolable, and it takes upon itself the transcendent qualities of the Absolute. Armed with this reaffirmation of life, the seeker's purpose in life has become profoundly renewed and regenerated. The seeker has thus received the boon, the gift of grace that reinvigorates and inspires anew the seeker's direction and quest for truth.

The boon actually consists of a vision that imparts a special knowledge to the seeker. This vision is a revelation of the Cosmic Cycle, which shows the entire life span of the world, from its creation to its final dissolution. The symbolic progression of this cycle is realized in the physical and historical processes of our own world. The seeker is shown the place that he occupies in this historical progression, and thereby gains an understanding of his future destiny and purpose.

Part III - The Cosmogonic Cycle[25]

The Cosmogonic Cycle unrolls the great vision of creation and destruction of the world that is granted as a revelation to the successful hero. The vision is revealed as the boon, which is the goal of the heroic quest.

0. World Navel; the Central Origin of All Things (Atu: XXI - The Universe)

The background of the Cycle of Initiation and the Cosmic Cycle is the ever preexistent source of all that was, is and will be. The Source of all things is the principal provider of all manifestation, the grace of the emanations of the Spirit and its role as that which sustains all manifestation. The Cycle of Initiation reaffirms the placement and importance of the Source and reestablishes its effectiveness from the diminishment that necessitated the advent of the threshold crossing. The individual as well as the world draws from this resource and when it is obstructed, all manifestation perishes.

The place where the Source dispenses its bounty is the very center of being itself, the invisible yet always present source of good and evil, life and death. It can be symbolized as the World Tree, the World Mountain, the Ladder of Lights, the Limitless Well of Souls and by other symbols. However, this Eternal Source and the relationship that all manifested nature has with it, represents the hidden, basic motif of the Cosmic Cycle, as well as the Cycle of

---

[25]   See *Hero with a Thousand Faces* by Joseph Campbell - p.40 - 48, 255 - 378

Initiation of the individual. All things have their origin in the Eternal Source, and all things return to it when their life cycle has ended.

1. Emanations; Emergence from the Void (Atu: XVII - The Star)

From the background of Eternal Night, which is the domain of the Eternal Source, emerges the first principle of Creation. As this creative effort moves from the highest levels of being to the lowest, the emergence of consciousness presages the evolution of physical life. The first principle is the Light or the Logos, the intelligible will to act and create. The first principle is not eternal, for it also has a beginning and an end. However, the eternal twilight world of the Source remains forever.

The first emanation is represented by the passage of individual consciousness out of the collective unconscious source. The origin of all beings is steeped in dreamlike mythic images that defy translation, buried as they are in the fabric of creation itself. This process of emanation has its representation in the human psyche, as the passage from deep sleep to waking has its intermediary in the manifestation of dreams.

2. Virgin Birth; Creative Roles of Women and the Mythical Golden Age (Atu: III - The Empress)

The first principal emanation requires a transforming medium so that the potential residing in the Source can become the actualized product of Creation. That transforming medium in numerous guises was the great Mother Goddess, the primal mediatrix who was instrumental in the release of the creative emanations from the Source. The unmanifest is drawn out of its complacency by the magnetic powers of the feminine, thus the medium of transformation becomes the womb of the Virgin Birth, the creation of life directly from the unmanifest.

The first Creation becomes the pattern by which all else is modeled, and it represents the archetypal patterns that imprint all creation. The archetypal level is symbolized by the Golden Age of Greek myth or the Paradise of the Garden of Eden. In this place there is no decay, change or birth. All the potential that will ever be has already been formulated, for there is no change in Paradise, only the interplay of various archetypes.

3. *Transformation; the Age of Death and Suffering (Atu: XIII - Death)*

Creative archetypes manifest the world of physical forms and organic being, giving it structure and a sense of order. The merging of consciousness and physical life represents the activating powers of transformation that are inherent in physical manifestation. For herein there is birth, life, corruption, decay and ultimately, death. The physical world is continuously changing, and the spirit that is locked in matter must learn to master the process of transformation in order to complete its spiritual process of evolution. Here is the paradox; that as physical matter corrupts and decays it brings forth new life to replenish itself as a whole. The Egregore of life resides in the consciousness of its individual parts, and these may experience a psychic evolution within a single manifestation, sharing in the collective fate of the group. Thus there are two processes at work simultaneously, the action of entropy on physical matter and the action of synergy on the part of consciousness.

The Age of Death is also represented by the age of history, the time of human endeavors and accomplishments. History is the process of emanation as it manifests through the space-time continuum, and it highlights the godlike accomplishments of the human spirit. As beings of flesh and spirit, we are forever shifting, changing and seeking, searching for that which represents for us the eternal purpose of existence, the Atman or God/dess-Within.

4. *Dissolutions; the End of the World (Atu: XII - The Hanged Man)*

The fate of all physical manifestation is dissolution, termination in death and disorder. For many, it is the only moment where the individual becomes aware of the transcendental process, the imposition of the supernatural upon the mortal connection of flesh and spirit. Herein the power of transformation reaches its final goal, the end of change and the return to the archetypal level of existence. The descent of spirit into matter is analogous to the ascent of consciousness into union with its source. Thus both evolution and incarnation partake in the synthesis of spirit and matter.

The ending of life represents the return to a higher level, and this is the mystery of the dying God, the sacrifice of divinity for the sake of the spiritual immortality of humanity. The individual conscious human spirit, which is unfettered by the limitations of physical existence, progresses from conscious awareness to superconscious via the transcendental process. Therefore, the stage of dissolution is yet another form of transformation, a symbol for the end result of spiritual evolution, which is enlightenment and total at-one-ment.

Part IV - The Return and Reintegration with Society[26]

1. The Refusal to Return; the World Denied, the Completion of the Path of the Mystic (Atu: VIII - Justice)

The attainment of the boon and the metamorphosis of the seeker still requires a return to the mundane world. It is customary for the cycle of the inward and outward pathways to be completed by a corresponding return from the depths of the inner-world of the collective unconscious. However, some paths to enlightenment (especially those that are mystical) don't need to make the final return circuit. The attainment of the blessing of the Deity is all that is required of the individual seeker, and having renounced the physical world, he lives in the world of the spirit and never returns.

For the magician the cycle must be completed so that the wisdom of the inner-worlds is able to regenerate and restore the purpose and beliefs of the outer world. The seeker who completes the cycle must now confront the issues that prevent the return, and they are associated with the tasks of translating the knowledge of the boon into the language of the everyday world.

2. The Magic Flight; Escape/Crossing the Return Threshold (Atu: XVIII - The Moon)

The return cycle has its own associated resistance and trials that the seeker must undergo. The pristine state of accomplishment is followed by the darkness and pain associated with the rebirth and reintegration of the newly formulated self back into the mundane world. There is another threshold to be crossed and it has a guardian at its gate similar to the guardian of the threshold of the entrance way. Thus there are obstructions and potential self-betrayal in the process of reintegrating with the physical self, and the seeker must hold fast to what is true rather than what is illusory.

---

[26]   See *Hero with a Thousand Faces* by Joseph Campbell – p.193 - 243

3. Rescue from Without; the Healing of the Fisher King (Atu: IV - The Emperor)

The seeker may require assistance or mediation to complete the task of reintegration. The process of mediation consists of the affirmations that link the World of the Spirit with the world of humanity. That mediation is the communion of spirit within and without the flesh. Throughout the inner journey of the spirit of the inner self, the outward self has been an automaton, acting without the inspiration or the intuition of the soul, being merely a cog in the machine of social intercourse. The process of reintegration consists of the realization of the sacredness of physical conscious existence and the return of the spirit to the flesh.

The seeker is awakened by a profound occurrence, which is the question that heralds the return of the spiritual dimension amidst the drudgery of mundane existence. The return is precipitated by the desire to know and the asking of the fateful question by either the seeker or some intermediary: "Who am I?" The answer is self-determining (I am a Man and more) and reestablishes the meaning of the inner journey, thus translating the vision into the beliefs and mythic motifs of the society of which one is still a part. The act of interpretation causes the message to lose something of its original purity. Thus it will eventually fail in its turn and have to be replaced in the trials of yet another inner journey.

4. The Reoccurrence of the Boon; the Expression of the World Redeeming Vision (Atu: XIV - Temperance)

The vision of the inner journey, which is the boon the seeker gained, integrates the inner and outer worlds. The vision presents the individual with his place in the process of the spiritual evolution of the world. It also reveals the knowledge of the place where each individual of all of humanity has a place in that divine plan. The message must be depersonalized and made to objectively express the purer forms of the archetypal level so that it is intelligible to others outside of the transformative process. The medium that this message may be expressed would consist of art rather than religion, and the cycle of initiation becomes a process by which the soul of humanity expresses its inner self through the palettes and canvas of painters, the clay, wax or wood of sculptors, the sonnets of poets, or the visions and beliefs of great leaders. The expression of the vision represents the creation of new values for a culture or society.

5. Master of Two Worlds; the Key to the Inner and Outer Realities (Atu V - The Hierophant)

Once the seeker has learned the mysteries that surround the processes of the inner and outer journey, the seeker then becomes a mediator for their continuous cycle. The ability to readily translate the experiences of the World of the Spirit into newly formed ideals and the ability to control the process of transformation resulting in the mastery that restores the meaning of life are the ideal achievements of the Cycle of Initiation.

This mastery is symbolized by the Hierophant who holds the keys to heaven and earth, thus "Whatever is loosed in heaven is loosed on earth," and "As above, so below." The person who has attained this mystery must bypass all the ephemeral pleasures of egocentric existence for the vocation of spiritual service. Therefore, having been reborn in the light of truth, the relevancy of personal gain and glory is ended. Such a person has become the pure instrument of the divine plan, the channel of the Absolute Spirit, as it communes with the nature of individual humanity.

6. Freedom to Live; the Function of the Ultimate Boon (Atu: XIX - The Sun)

The seeker who has resigned personal will, and gained the mediation of the Absolute Spirit, also receives the blessing of knowledge and the certainty of perfected faith. As an instrument of the divine, the seeker has been released from the bondage of all social and psychological restrictions and limitations and is completely liberated. There are no restrictions imposed on an individual who can easily travel between the inner and outer worlds, for what is not possible in one world is possible in the other.

The power of selfless actions and unworldly concerns are the domain of the enlightened seeker. Powerful insight and unencumbered actions represent the pure spiritual archetype manifested in the human body. This is the nature of the spiritual master, as well as the incarnated avatar. The quality of eternal renewal has as its essential nature that which never truly dies. It only changes its outer appearance and remains inviolable in cycles of eternal manifestation.

9.3 The Feminine Cycle of Initiation

The above Cycle of Initiation represents both the general mythic motif of self-transformation and the specific pattern of the masculine initiation cycle. There is a gender-specific initiation pattern for women, and it varies only somewhat from the masculine pattern. It will not be necessary to restate those elements they have in common. However, the following represents the points that differentiate the two cycles.

The feminine Cycle of Initiation is not as well known as the masculine cycle, and this should not be surprising given the emphasis in our culture on the masculine perspective. The feminine initiation cycle can be found in two particular mythic representations, the Descent of Innana (the Sumerian Goddess of Life) and the trials of Psyche in the mythic tale of Eros and Psyche. There are also a few folk tales where this motif is repeated, such as in the Scandinavian tale of East of the Sun and West of the Moon. The pattern of the cycle of feminine initiation has been deduced from these myths.

The feminine initiation cycle has four sections. These are the same as the masculine pattern, but the significance and ordering of each section of the feminine cycle is different, representing a different type of psychic ordeal. The visionary mystery plays a very important part in the feminine cycle, and so it is the first section in the feminine initiation pattern. The pattern begins with the Vision of the Mystery of the Body, then proceeds through the Marriage to Death and the Temptation of the Serpent of Knowledge, undergoing the Trials of Love, and is completed by the Daughter as Mother.[27]

The cycle begins with a woman realizing the creative shaping power inherent in her body that gives it the divine function of joining spirit to flesh in the birth of new life. The newly discovered powers of womanhood are put into perspective by society's devaluation of a woman's role and by her subsequent struggle against this tyranny. The temptation of the serpent represents the

---

[27]   See *She – Understanding Feminine Psychology* by Robert A. Johnson for an excellent study of the feminine cycle of transformation.

struggle of the feminine spirit against the shadow beast of the negative image of masculinity.

Empowerment of the feminine is accomplished through the inner knowledge of the self and the rediscovery of the creative powers inherent in all women. The trials of love represent the social techniques by which the knowledge of the feminine spirit, internally regained, is made manifest in the outer world.

The final section is where the feminine spirit is integrated into the world. It is where all women and men are drawn together through the sacrifice of unconditional love, and where occurs the merging of the mother and daughter archetypes of the feminine. This union produces the lineage of sacramental life.

Following is a detailed analysis of the previous sections of the feminine Initiation Cycle including the analogous Tarot Trumps that make up the stages of each section. Keep in mind, the definitions of the stages do not differ much from the stages defined in the masculine cycle, mentioned earlier. However, the feminine pattern of initiation differs from the masculine in that some sections use very different stages than the masculine, thus altering the context of their meanings.

1. The Body of Woman as Avatar (The Visionary Mystery)
(Atus: XXI, VII, XIX, IV, XVII)

A woman has a natural alignment to her spiritual nature through her body, whereas a man tries to find this same connection in his mind. The center of this power is, of course, the heart, which represents the role of the feminine as the transformative power of love and compassion that holds human society together. A body-centered spirituality does not negate the faculty of the mind. Instead it allows for the natural and harmonious integration of the mind and body to prevail over other perspectives. Therefore, women have an innate sense of harmony in nature, which is reinforced through the menstrual cycle and their power of creation.

The source of this mystery is represented by the same stage and Tarot trump as in the masculine cycle, which is the World (Atu: XXI). But the occurrence of the creative emanations, which is the second stage, are experienced as the essence of life and the power of ecstasy (Atu: VII). The Golden Age, which is the third stage, was a time when the feminine was revered for its power of creativity, when men deferred to women for their creative and healing magic and could not rule without their consent (Atu: XIX). The Age of Death, which is the fourth stage, is represented by the current social circumstance of a male-dominated society. This dominance betrays a great weakness and a troubling imbalance in society (Atu: IV). The dissolution, which is the final stage, is represented by the ascendancy of the feminine spirit (the Star) and the associated social phenomenon of the renewal of women's spirituality (Atu XVII). The stage of dissolution is actually where the imbalance of the current age is corrected, so it does not represent an ending of the world, it represents a great beginning or renewal.

2. The Marriage to Death and the Temptation of the Serpent
(Atus: XX, 0, II, VI, XIII)

The beginning of the initiation pattern for women is the same as that for men (Atu: XX, Atu: 0 and Atu: II), differing only when the threshold is achieved. This is because the promising potential of life experienced in childhood, which occurs for both boys and girls, is discouraged for the young woman because of the inherent devaluation of the feminine in our society (Atu: VI). Whether a woman chooses to adapt and play the inferior role that some men expect or to aggressively pursue her goals as does a man, there is a price to be paid, namely the loss of the feminine soul. This entails a loss of innocence as well as a loss of self-esteem. Thus women are faced with the choice of being either like Eve or Lilith, the good mother or the evil courtesan, but not both at the same time.

The resolution of this issue is to present both sides of the dynamic as a whole process, instead of being split into two qualities. The path of Eve is analogous to the Marriage to Death (Atu: XIII), in which the woman has given up her dreams in order to raise a family. The path of Lilith is analogous to the Temptation of the Serpent, in which a woman abandons her feminine power of creation in order to pursue her personal ambitions. However, the women of the Bronze Age city-states of the Aegean were uniquely able to assume both dynamics at the same time and did not have to depend on a man for economic support. Therefore, it is not only possible for a woman to integrate both paths, but its part of a woman's ancient heritage to be able to do so.

This section has the same stages as the masculine cycle except that the stages of the Threshold and the Underworld are held by the Trumps of the Lovers and Death, respectively. These two stages demonstrate that women are polarized by their choices in life and denied the ability to make a decision based upon their actual desires and aspirations. However, what is sacrificed always finds its way into the unconscious mind, and there the deflected part of a woman's personality is left to cause problems later on.

3. *The Trials of Love (Atus: X, XV, XI, XII, VIII, XIV)*

The Trials of Love (Atu: X) represent the process in which a woman initiate struggles with the problems of self-definition and self-emancipation. To facilitate adaption to a male-dominated society, the part of the personality that has been discarded will take on a mind and a life of its own, becoming the shadow being of the woman (Lilith). Other possible forms include a dark, repressed and negative masculine archetype (Atu: XV - The Devil) or an alter ego of the woman (man within) ready to flood her emotions with self-destructive impulses. The actual issue for the woman initiate is the wresting of personal freedom related to issues concerning her body and her reproductive potential from a male-dominated society. There is also the need to apply the power of truth to the alliances of the heart and weigh each against the need for personal power and emancipation. Only when the discarded part of the self is recognized and reintegrated into the identity of the woman initiate will this ordeal be considered complete.

The Trials of Love differ dramatically from the corresponding masculine cycle. The lesser trials are all lessons that teach a woman the need to control her body in order to control her fate. The Supreme Ordeal is represented by the card of the Devil, in which the woman initiate must confront her discarded part that assumes the persona of the negative masculine. The issue of Strength (Atu: XI) is the same as with the masculine cycle, but the method of resolving the Supreme Ordeal and gaining self-mastery is different.

The woman initiate must detach momentarily from her emotions (Adjustment, Atu: VIII), in order to adjust her personal spiritual alignment. The ordeal is represented by a personal self-sacrifice (the Hanged Man, Atu: XII). This is the power that evokes a woman's strong instinctual reflex to protect a child or loved one from harm even at the cost of her own life. This power can be used in a very constructive manner, assisting a woman initiate in establishing her boundaries and giving her the strength to determine her own destiny. The final outcome of the ordeal

(Temperance, Atu: XIV) is the mastery of the art of communicating the needs, goals and desires of her inner self through her identity to society. This mastery will cause her to make profound changes in the world, which will enable her to act in the most creative and productive manner possible.

4. The Daughter as Mother (Atus: XVI, XVIII, III, IX, V, I)

The final section of the women's initiation cycle consists of the struggle to create a new social order, both from the standpoint of the individual and society at large. The changes that the woman initiate has undergone have been internalized, causing her to be empowered and whole. Thus she is able to realize the most important goal, the passing of a new social order on to her younger sisters and daughters, brothers and sons, and bearing the torch of knowledge so that they will be equally empowered and individually valued. The woman initiate is now able to turn her attention to the most difficult issues --women who resist change and who are still polarized by the dichotomy of Eve and Lilith. These women, who are not yet whole and healed, will be a greater threat to the movement of feminine spirituality than overly defensive and conservative men. However, the final outcome has already been decided. A long period of resistance may delay the changes and may attempt to prevent them, but the age of equity and equality is coming and nothing can prevail against it.

The stages of the final section are also very different from the masculine cycle. The Tower trump (Atu: XVI) represents the need for a change in the social order, but The Moon trump (Atu: XVIII) represents the possibility of a backlash and a betrayal from within. The Empress trump (Atu: III) represents the final outcome of this initiation process on both the individual and the collective level. The power of creation and the forces of nature will be respected and revered once again, but this time there will be greater knowledge and wisdom in its control and use. The Hermit, the Hierophant and the Magus trumps (Atus: IX, V and I, respectively) represent the final transformation of the woman initiate once she has completed the process of integration, followed by a period of retirement (internalization) from the concerns of life and death. She becomes the mistress of the mysteries of death, rebirth and the magick of metamorphosis. This final transformation occurs only after the worldly concerns of the woman initiate have been turned over to younger and stronger hands and she is left free to pursue the inner paths of a higher spirituality of life: the preparation for death and rebirth in the life of the community.

9.4 Lesser Initiation Cycle of Self-Actualization

We now turn to another topic related to the transformative cycle of initiation -- the methods of self-actualization and personal change that characterize what I call the lesser cycle of initiation.

While the greater initiation cycles of the hero and heroine represent large-scale changes in the individual, another mechanism represents the smaller changes that are needed in order to undergo the greater ones. The smaller changes involve psychological processes called individuation and self-actualization.

Individuation is a word coined by C. G. Jung to explain the process whereby an individual is emancipated from the slavery of social consensus and becomes truly self-aware. Self-actualization is a concept that was invented by Abraham Maslow and represents the full development of the self that only occurs after all the basic needs of survival have been sufficiently met. Both of these concepts represent the state that we strive to achieve, which is the overcoming of all personal barriers.

While there are a number of mechanisms and techniques to stimulate individuation and self-actualization, only one appears to use the cycle of initiation. This is a tool of direct conscious reprogramming, and it is a proven tool that a magician can use for complete self-determination.

This technique is found in the psychological self-help system known as Holodynamics, which was developed by V. Vernon Woolf, Ph.D. It is called Tracking.[28] This technique has a six-part progression that assists seekers in accessing, resolving and evolving the archetypal complex that represents their problem or issue.

According to Holodynamics, the archetypal complex is the heart or core of all problems and issues, and is called a holodyne because it represents a dynamic psychic process. The concept of an archetype has always had the connotation of being a static two-dimensional object instead of a transmuting, changing and three-dimensional process. The word holodyne better captures the characteristics of psychological dynamics. The holodyne is the key to personal transformation and the resolving of personal difficulties.

---

[28]   See *Holodynamics* by V. Vernon Woolf Ph.D., 1990, Harbinger House)

The basic premise of tracking is that it transforms the holodyne at the center of an issue, and so removes personal barriers and obstacles to the achievement of individuation and self-actualization. Until the development of Tracking by Dr. Woolf, no method of psychology has ever presented a simple method that would allow one to achieve self-actualization or individuation. It seems that the biggest obstacles to self-actualization are embedded deep within, and the best tool with which to attack these problems is one that can directly access those inner problem areas.

The mind is dominated by visual images and words, so the psyche functions like a visual processor. By using methods of visualization, psychologists have had some success in treating mental disorders. But these methods were limited by the psychological theories of behavior that had dictated their use as a means of therapy.

Patients engaged in a visualization technique called free association that allowed them to talk about whatever entered into their mind, and this was analyzed by the physician for the benefit of the patient. However, analysis and talk therapies do not enter the deeper layers of the psyche where the holodynes live.

Change at the level of the holodyne allows for transformation that is rapid and permanent. Behavior changes automatically when it is internally motivated and self-directed. Behavior that is modified by force, punishment or manipulation from the outside by suggestion, drugs, or mechanical means is temporary and does not cause changes in the deeper and more permanent levels of the self.

This powerful technique of visualization was severely handicapped when systems of therapy allowed for the subjugation of the methodology by the theory of behavior. To use the method of visualization to its fullest capability, one must first be free of any model or expectation, then to directly identify and personify problems using fantasy as a means to conduct a dialogue with one's self. In this fashion, one may quickly use the inherent capabilities of the mind to perform psychic diagnostics and discover the internal characteristics of one's mind.

This useful and temporary fragmentation of the ego in various parts or roles is not harmful. It is not, however, viewed with any sympathy or encouragement by those who represent the established psychotherapeutic disciplines. However, the advent of the New Age has given considerable recognition to the beneficial uses of visualization. Dr. Woolf's method of tracking has brought the technique of visualization into the foreground and he has shown it to be the primary technique of healing and self-improvement.

I have practiced and used this technique, demonstrating the powers inherent in visualization. The reason why it is such a powerful technique is that the six stages of tracking used in *Holodynamics*,[29] is an archetypal pattern familiar to all who know the cycle of the Hero. I was able to match the six stages of tracking to the twenty-two stages of the Cycle of Initiation. Each of the six stages of tracking can be compared to one or several of the twenty-two stages of initiation.

The Cycle of Initiation is used to understand the potent transformational event in the spiritual life of an individual. The system of tracking is used to resolve personal problems and free one's self from psychic obstructions. The only difference between these two methodologies is one of scale.

Tracking is a process that is used with greater frequency and initiation occurs only after an extended period of spiritual growth. The effect of continually addressing one's issues facilitates the maximizing of one's personal potential, and this hastens the frequency of the performance of initiation rites.

The use of tracking as one of two methods facilitating spiritual growth seems to represent a forgotten part of the Cycle of Initiation. The similarity between these two patterns is too striking to be considered coincidental. The Cycle of Initiation, in addition to marking the greater passages of the initiate, was probably applied to resolving individual problems, thus allowing for the clearing of the mind and soul for higher spiritual developments.

The techniques of Holodynamics represent a new version of an ancient method for the promotion of individual growth and ultimate enlightenment. For practicing occultists, it represents the rediscovery of an important part of the initiation cycle. This rediscovery will greatly facilitate the process of spiritual evolution within the Western Mystery tradition.

When tracking is applied within a magickal ritual, a powerful tool of transformation is wielded. However, the reader is encouraged to purchase Dr. Woolf's book and gain a greater understanding of his methodologies. The following section does little justice to his unique insights and theories and was written as a

---

[29]   See *Holodynamics* by V. Vernon Woolf Ph.D., p. 40 - 42

brief comparison, highlighting the important concepts for applying the Cycle of Initiation to the process of empowering one's full potential.

The following section is a brief comparison between the two systems of tracking and the cycle of initiation, demonstrating in what manner they are alike.

Contrast Between Tracking and the Cycle of Initiation

1. **Access the Holodyne:** The first step in tracking is to identify the problem and its various associations. This is represented in the cycle of initiation by the Call to Adventure (Atu: XX - The Aeon), wherein the challenge to the individual is realized. Once the problem is identified, a guide is sought to mediate it, and through mediation the responsible holodyne is located. The search for a Guide is analogous to Supernatural Intervention (Atu: II - The Priestess) that leads the initiate to the source or core of the self that is symbolized by the House of God (Atu: XVI - the Tower). The responsible holodyne is symbolized by the Crossing of the Threshold (Atu: IX - The Hermit) that represents the power to transmute experiences from both without and within.

2. **Befriend the Holodyne:** The next step is to communicate with the holodyne and find out what it has been doing within your psyche, allowing the holodyne to relate its story and thus reveal its goal. The problem is really an opportunity for growth, and this is analogous to the initiation process known as the Lesser Trials (Atu: X - The Wheel of Fortune). The trial that an initiate endures reveals his/her true inner nature, thus allowing for a greater self-awareness.

3. **Transform the Holodyne into its Mature Image:** The third step is to seek out the holodyne in its resolved phase or mature state. One attempts to imagine the holodyne as it would appear as an adult, fully developed and actualized. Then one compares the mature state to the original state and traces backwards the steps required to fulfill the holodyne in its immature state. This process is analogous to the Supreme Ordeal (Atu: VI - The Lovers) wherein the initiate becomes integrated through the joining of the light and dark aspects of him/herself. The integration must be balanced, thus a second process is involved in the stage of the cycle of initiation,

Temptation (Atu: XI - Strength), in which the Light and Darkness must be carefully balanced so that neither dominates and so obscures the integrated self.

4. **Create Internal Order:** In the fourth step, one seeks the teaching necessary to completely resolve its associated issue from the mature holodyne. This stage is analogous to three stages in the initiation cycle. The first stage is the process where the basis of self integration is given a permanent structure through the establishment of a discipline, represented by Atonement (Atu: XIII - The Devil). The second stage is the process in which the structure of balanced integration allows the self to realize its wholeness as expressed by the Higher Self, thus one becomes the Apotheosis (Atu: I - The Magician). The third stage is the realization of one's true identity brought on by the understanding of one's spiritual purpose and direction, and how they link with the larger cycle of the world. Thus the third initiatory stage is the discovery of the Boon (Atu: VII - The Chariot). This process requires a renewal of one's spiritual dedication that seals the relationship between the self and Higher Self.

5. **Establish a Principal Perspective:** The fifth step is where all that has been learned and previously established is translated into one's daily existence. This is the real test, where the mature holodyne must exert its influence and ultimately integrate with its immature counterpart through the persistent efforts of the individual through frequent inner consultations and contacts to ensure a permanent change and a resultant progression to the next stage of development. This step is analogous to the entire initiation process called The Return, and thus represents six stages of Initiation that assist the seeker to reintegrate the vision gained within the World of the Spirit into the mundane world, thus restoring it.

6. **Universalize:** The sixth and final step is to apply the knowledge gained through integrating the mature holodyne successfully into the sphere of one's individual's life and applying it to the analogous problems of one's neighborhood, town or even the nation and world. The knowledge gained through one's individual dynamic process is recursive and applicable at other levels than the individual. This is analogous to the occult concept that was

established by the teachings of Hermes the Thrice Great: "That which is above is like that which is below, and that which is below is like that which is above." This is the Cosmic Cycle or the Vision as the heroic boon that is represented in the Cycle of Initiation by five stages, symbolized by Creation, the Golden Age, the Age of Humanity and Death, the Dissolution and the Center that never changes. This Cosmic Cycle is applicable at various scales, both on the level of the individual, as well as the level of the Universe

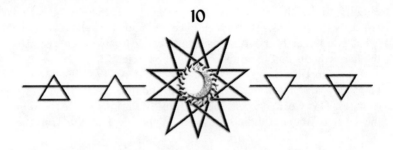

10

The Five Mystery Systems

We have covered the various elements of ritual magick, discussed the process of transformative initiation, and briefly mentioned the mystery rites of the Sun and Moon. In the following text, we will explore the mysteries in greater detail, since they represent the core of an intermediate magickal discipline.

If the expression of magick in the natural world is reflected in the mysteries of that world, then knowledge of those mysteries would be essential to understanding magick and how they affect the world. While one could easily conceive of a myriad of mysteries and devote an entire work to that subject, we need only to cover the basic set of mysteries that concern the practicing magician.

I believe that there are five mystery systems as defined in the earth-based spiritual traditions of Neopaganism and Witchcraft, which are chief amongst the targeted religions for this work. These five mystery systems represent the types and characteristics of transcendental magick that are practiced in those earth-based spiritual traditions.

The mysteries are simply stated as:

* *Cycle of Day and Night (Light and Darkness)*
* *Lunar cycle*
* *Solar cycle*
* *Cycle of Birth, Life, Death and individual transcendence (initiation)*
* *Paradoxical nature of Spirit and Deity.*

As you can see, I did not pick five as an arbitrary number of the mysteries. I truly believe that there are five mysteries found in the rediscovered pagan religious traditions.

The mystery rites of earth-based spiritual traditions are represented by the liturgical symbols and ritual expressions that not only forge an alignment with the Deity, as is done in exoteric forms of Christianity, but realize that Deity intimately within one's self.

Followers of these spiritual traditions seek to understand the intrinsic nature of Deity and how it operates in the world. So for them the mysteries involve the Deity and how it manifests itself into the world of matter.

Deity is a part of the material world, and this fact allows initiates to have intimate relationships with that Deity. The mysteries involve the various periodic cycles of change in the world, of Light and Darkness, Life and Death, representing the effect of Deity acting through that world. Thus the Deity is perceived as acting as an integral and essential part of the world.

The mysteries are the apprehension, realization, and inspiration of profoundly deep spiritual transformations that occur in a cyclic fashion to all human life. They are events that must be experienced in order to be realized and understood. The mysteries are powerful transformations that can impact a single person or an entire group simultaneously.

These five mystery systems could be readily symbolized by the Pentagram. This would make the pentagram itself a symbol of the Mysteries -- a sixth mystery (the mystery of Phi). There are obviously many more mysteries aside from these, but for this study, we shall examine only the five stated above.

Mysteries, expressed as liturgical mechanisms (magickal rituals), are performed by individuals and groups in order to become aware of one's self within the domains of Spirit and Nature. The mysteries are transcendental occurrences that must be faced in order to be realized.

Since Spirit transcends the domain of the mind and language, the mysteries have the quality of being inexplicable. Experience is the key to understanding and knowing the intrinsic nature of all things that are of spirit, mind, body and the world.

Spiritual knowledge is the foundation of faith, and is superior in all ways to mere belief, which does not require experiential knowledge or wisdom to sustain itself. Experience leads to knowing that is a permanent change in the self, which is an adaption to a new way of perceiving and behaving in the world.

Spiritual knowledge is the perceptual intuition of Spirit in terms of how it acts and relates to the individual and the world at large, so that quality of perceptual intuition can be considered Gnosis. Experience and adaption together are the tools of the seeker and represent the manner in which an immanent spiritual tradition should function for the practitioner.

Meditation and ritual magick are the mechanisms that produce spiritual experiences within the traditions of Witchcraft and Neopaganism. These mechanisms are not used to behold an outer and unapproachable Deity nor to bolster a groundless doctrine of beliefs. They realize and adapt to a perspective where Deity, Spirit, and the individual person are in perfect and indivisible union. The practices of these new religious systems are quite different than their monotheistic predecessors, which are Judaism, Christianity and Islam.

Change as Light and Darkness

These five mystery systems are based on the cycles of constant change that are perceived in the world and within one's self. These mysteries are based upon the apparent operation of these cycles of change, and are imbued with a greater significance and meaningfulness than would otherwise be perceived, since they are an integral part of the life on this planet Earth.

The constant changes involve the diurnal cycle of day and night, the twenty-eight day cycle of the Moon, the 365 day cycle of the Sun, the four Seasons, the life-cycle of all living things, and the internal transformative process of the individual. In addition, there is also the mystery of the nature and essential quality of Deity itself, where it is perceived as a distinct being or a multitude of beings, each with its own qualities and characteristics. It also is perceived in a non-dual fashion, as an expression of a unified whole that is Spirit.

In addition to the constant changes in nature, there are also catastrophic changes, accidental deaths, epidemics, and the natural predation between species and within species. Yet despite the constant changes, as well as the catastrophic ones, which permanently alter the world in which we live, human nature progresses through a set life cycle that has an apparent beginning (birth) and an end (death), a thing that it shares with all creatures that live and thrive on this planet.

These cycles represent a process of duality based on the diurnal nature of planetary motion, but what is operating cannot be perceived as anything except a continuum of change. Life and death, light and darkness merge one into the other, and they have no separation except by contrast. So there is no intrinsic value for this duality of life and death, light and darkness, and one can't judge them as being either good or evil. They just exist!

It is a prerequisite of monotheistic religions to give values to light and darkness, life and death, to label one good, and the other evil, and claim that this duality is in constant warfare. However, these phenomena have no intrinsic values. It is a folly to value life and light as good, and darkness and death as evil. Nothing could be further from the truth, especially when we objectively observe nature. There is no good and evil in the phenomena of nature. Our perception of good and evil is based on what we judge as being either beneficial or detrimental to our lives. This is quite subjective and can vary from individual to individual and culture to culture.

Everything is a manifestation of a single unified expression of being, existing in an illimitable vortex of change. It is wrapped up into a seamless holism of matter, mind and spirit.

If we are to apprehend spirituality as it truly exists, and to evolve beyond belief systems that do not allow questions, individualization, self determination, and the adoption of new realizations, then we must abandon the bankrupt myths and closed belief systems of the past and embrace, with an open mind, the natural world that we live in.

We will not find spirit outside of ourselves, nor will we find it outside of the natural world where we exist. We will find it within ourselves first, and then in nature, especially nature that is untrammeled by the human hand.

Change occurs in two manners within human consciousness -- translation and transformation. Translation represents the outer changes that occur which do not intrinsically change a thing. Transformation is change that alters something deep within, shifting its essential definition. Thus translation represents a surface change and transformation represents change at a fundamental level. Transformation causes changes within a person's psychic deep structure, changing the innate definition of their entire being.

The mysteries represent changes that are translations and transformations, occurring both within the individual and in the world at large. These changes also represent an evolution of spirit and mind traveling through the changing world of matter and existence.

Mystery of Day and Night

The primary cycle associated with the mysteries is the cycle of day and night. The definition of a single day is the occurrence of a cyclic period of 24 hours. This period is the building block of our sense of the passage of time. The revolution of light and darkness that create day and night are intrinsic to human nature, since we cycle from sleep to wakefulness and back again to sleep every twenty-four hours.

In daylight we are fully functional and active, at night, we complete our tasks and adjourn to sleep. In between this diurnal cycle of night and day, sleep and wakefulness, we dream, fantasize, and create worlds and realities with our minds. These places and events that have no reality in the waking world but are usually derived from them in some fashion. The common occurrence of day and night is not the mystery, but our response to it. Therefore, the revelation of worlds of dream and fantasy represent the first mystery.

Lunar Mystery

The next cycle associated with the mysteries is the cycle of the Moon, the twenty-eight[30] day cycle where the Moon passes through its four phases, from New, to First Quarter, to Full, to Last Quarter, and finally again to New moon.

This astronomical phenomenon is not at all mysterious, since it is readily explained as the effect perceived by people on earth seeing the illuminated half of the moon from various perspectives, depending on the viewing geometry of the moon relative to the earth and sun. However, the effect of this constant lunar change, from new, to full and back again, does have a powerful effect on the human psyche. Each full moon during a month has a seasonal quality and mythology, as does the astrological quality of that full moon. There is the symbology of the lunation cycle, and there are

---

[30] The average of the synodic month (29.5 days) and the sidereal month (27.3 days) 28 days.

also the mansions of the moon, and all of these qualities add to the occult perspectives of the entire lunar cycle that occurs every month.

The moon represents qualities that are the opposite of the sun, and where it also functions as a luminary in the sky, it appears most dramatically during the night, when it has its greatest effect. The moon shining in the night symbolizes the light that subtly illuminates the darkness, creating many illusions and strange shadows as it reveals the contours of the landscape hidden by the night. The moon's illumination is spectral, representing the world as it is perceived in the unconscious mind --full of mystery and pervaded by strange fantasies.

Such an environment is ideal for seekers who wish to know the nature of their hidden and inner self. So the night and lunar magick assists them in determining the nature and the topology of the deep structure of the self. It also reveals the shared myths of their culture, geographic location and the time where they all live.

Solar Mystery

The sun has its own cycle. This cycle determines the duration of the year as the 365-day period in which the earth makes its orbital sweep around the sun. Yet from our perspective on earth, it is the sun that makes this transition.

In reality there are two processes at work to cause an apparent change of season. First, it's the elliptical orbit around the sun that determines how close the earth is to the sun. Secondly, the fixed tilting of the earth's axis determines how much sunlight shines on either the northern or southern hemispheres. These phenomena cause the amount of light from the sun to vary as the earth circles around it, producing both the phenomena of shorter and longer days and the changing of the seasons in the temperate regions of the Earth.

When the earth's northern polar axis is tilted toward the sun, then summer and warmer weather ensues in the northern latitudes, while winter and colder weather ensues in the southern latitudes. When the earth's northern polar axis is tilted away from the sun, then winter and colder weather occurs in the northern latitudes, while summer and warmer weather occurs in the southern latitudes.

These two processes are really derived from the same phenomena. There is the phenomenon caused by the tilted axis and

173

the orbital position of the earth relative to the sun that determines the season. There is also the annual solar cycle, which is perceived as the transit of the sun through the twelve zodiacal signs situated at the celestial equator.

While it is actually the earth that is making this transit around the sun, from the perspective of astrology, the sun appears to move through the zodiac, making a complete cycle approximately every 365 days. This annual cycle through the twelve signs of the zodiac and the changing seasons, represent the two aspects of the solar cycle and its associated mysteries - the changing seasons, the waxing and waning of light, and the life cycle of vegetation that are subject to these variations.

In the latitudes that are distant from the earth's equator there is a noticeable difference between the changing of the seasons and the waxing and waning of light from the sun. The Summer Solstice represents the longest period of daylight during the year, and every day thereafter the days become shorter in relation to the nights.

However, it is not until just before the Autumn equinox, more than three months after the Summer Solstice that the seasons noticeably begin to change from summer to autumn. The same is true for the Winter Solstice. The days after the Winter Solstice are getting longer, but the season does not change from winter to spring until after the spring equinox.

In some latitudes, the season of spring does not become apparent until almost the month of May or later. So one could perceive the growing season as being somewhat displaced from the actual solar cycle. In the higher northern and southern latitudes, this observation is correct. For this reason, we could separate the growth cycle from the solar cycle and see it as two cycles that are inter-related but not equivalent.

As previously indicated, the solar cycle has four distinct nodes --the two solstices and the two equinoxes. The sun proceeds on its apparent journey through the annual cycle, and the duration of daylight waxes to its climactic event at the Summer Solstice, and then starts to wane until it reaches its point of greatest diminishment at the Winter Solstice. The equinoxes determine the points during the year where the period of daylight is balanced against the night, but where either the light is in its ascendancy or decline.

The four solar events represent the transition of the periodicity of daylight vs. night, and also represent the four seasons in their transition from one season to the next. These four solar events are concerned with the powers of light and darkness, and represent the transformative forces active in each of the four seasons.

The vegetative life cycle also occurs during the four seasons, and these events are marked by four periods that represent the fullness of each of those seasons. These four events occur in between the solstices and the equinoxes, and represent the state of the life cycle of vegetation, which also is emulated by all living things in one manner or another. Thus there is birth, growth, maturity and death, symbolizing the growing cycle of Spring, Summer, Autumn, and Winter.

These four seasonal events are concerned with the powers of life and death, and so are considered to be influenced by forces that are chthonic and aligned to the deepest structure existing in all living things. To those who live and must eventually die, the cycle of life and death is considered the greatest of all mysteries. The human life cycle consists of the mysteries of birth, puberty, procreation, maturity (aging) and death. This life cycle and its mysteries are echoed in various manners in all living things.

Initiation Mystery

The spiritual seeker has an internal cycle as well, and this cycle is in addition to the cycle of the moon, sun and the seasons, and the cycle of life and death. This cycle can actually be dormant in some individuals and barely perceived by others, but when activated, its dynamism drives one to be a spiritual seeker.

This cycle is the dynamic interaction of a person's conscious and unconscious mind, where the unconscious holds all of the potential within a human being, and the conscious mind represents all that is actualized within the self. A person never remains static, and the dynamic state that exists between the light and dark halves of the self can cause both surface and deep structure changes within that being.

This cycle of the self traveling into the unconscious and emerging into the consciousness mind is symbolized by the archetypal journey through the underworld, which we covered in the previous section. This is where the self undergoes the ordeal of disintegration and reintegration, and is seemingly reborn into the light of consciousness once again.

There are two gateways in this cycle, the gateway of death and the gateway of life, the double gateway of self transformation and regeneration. It is known in literature as the Hero's Journey, but it is really also the cycle of transformative initiation.

The light and dark cycle in the self is the greatest mechanism for realizing one's full-potential, but it's also the mechanism where the self can be destroyed by inner or outer forces, and where madness as well as genius can be realized.

The mystery of the cycle of initiation is the greatest mystery of the self, for it can resolve the fear and terror of death and oblivion. Through this cycle is the individual spirit revealed, and that realization can lead to illumination, and ultimately, full conscious union with one's God/dess Within.

Mystery of Deity

The final mystery does not represent a cycle per-se, but it could be considered the underlying spiritual process behind all of the cycles that a seeker might experience while practicing a spiritual and magickal discipline.

This mystery concerns the nature of Deity, and whether that Deity is defined as a distinct entity with specific qualities and characteristics, whether there is one or a multitude of these Deities, or whether Deity is perceived as being indistinguishable from the ground of Spirit from which it has its emanation.

Perhaps the greatest truth and paradox is that Deity can exist in any of these states, individually or simultaneously, and yet not exist in any of them. The definition of Deity cannot be adequately determined by the mind, so it can't be defined by a belief or a doctrine. Thus the Deity has one face, many faces, and no face at all. The paradox is that all of these statements are true.

Deity cannot be defined, but humans resist this limitation, so they will define the nature of Deity who is truly indefinable. This happens with use of images and characterizations that are based on human nature, and descriptions of the experience of the spiritual dimension using human values.

The most popular religions in the west propose a Deity that is monotheistic and outside of all material creation. However, one can see the absurdity of adhering to a doctrine of a single monotheistic concept of Deity, when human experience shows that Deity is multiform and intrinsic to all creation. Where the confusion arises is that Deity is also non-dual and transcendent.

Having covered the five mysteries, we shall now cover each of these mysteries in slightly greater detail, showing how they operate within the framework of a spiritual and magickal discipline as performed by one who is working through a Wiccan or Neopagan tradition. Ritual components that such a one would use to realize and experience these mysteries, and to integrate them into a practical discipline that fosters transformative initiation and the evolution of consciousness will also be examined.

10.1 Lunar Mystery

The features of this mystery are the waxing and waning of the Moon as it travels across the ecliptic of the zodiac. Each full moon occurs within the zodiacal sign opposite of the sun, and so each full moon has its own qualities and characteristics, as determined by the zodiacal sign and the season in which it occurs. Each phase of the moon has its own specific qualities, which can be determined by the Lunation Cycle and the Mansions of the Moon. The lunar cycle affects the changing of the tides and the cycle of fertility. The gravitational effect of the moon even stirs the core of the Earth as it makes its orbital circuit.

The moon has both a physical effect as well as a psychic effect on all living things, particularly more advanced mammals, and humankind. The lunar cycle symbolizes the inward and outward expression of the human mind, and its demarcation between consciousness and unconsciousness. The moon's psychic effects are best perceived during the night, when it is the brightest luminary in the sky. The lunar night represents the place where the inner worlds of the unconscious mind merge with the outer world of the conscious ego. When the two are merged, the latent possibilities in the self awaken and can become realized.

The magick performed during this mystery cycle represents the nature of the outer translations and inner transformations that affect the seeker, assisting in the realization of the domain of Spirit and the spiritual essence that lies deep within.

The Lunar Mystery is the mystery of Spirit embedded in life. The method and mechanisms that reveal that mystery are shrouded in the images, myths and occult symbology associated with the archetype of the Moon as it relates to the spiritual world. While the magickal discipline of the Moon is performed at least once a month when the moon is full, it can be expanded to include many other aspects of the moon too, depending on the kind of magick performed and the nature of the seeker's quest.

10.2 Solar Mystery

The solar mystery consists of the waxing and waning light of the sun, and duration of day opposed to the night. The mystery concerns itself with the entry of the sun into each of the twelve signs of the zodiac, as well as the four pivotal events of the solstices and the equinoxes.

The solar mystery specifically centers around the event of the solstices, when the spiritual aspect of the sun is perceived as dying and being reborn on the day of the Winter Solstice. The common event of the return of light is perceived as the miracle of the rebirth and regeneration of the sun. That death is but an illusion since the light unfailingly returns.

The myth of the sun passing through the solstices and equinoxes is not about a conflict between light and darkness, but a part of the natural process of the ascendancy and decline of light that is a part of all terrestrial existence.

The cycle of light and darkness reaches its maximum crisis or glory during the solstices, but achieves balance or parity during the equinoxes. The crisis or glorification is symbolized by a transformation of spirit into matter. The light dies and is reborn during the Winter Solstice, but the darkness gains an ascendency at the Summer Solstice.

The waxing and waning of light has a profound effect on the soul of mankind traveling through the solar season, causing one to become focused either on the outside world or inwardly (introspection). The colder the climate, the more inwardly focused one tends to become.

The projection of light is directed within the self during the autumn and winter, and directed outward during the spring and summer when temperatures beckon all living things to abandon their places of hibernation. This cycle of outer and inner focusing is highly celebrated by adherents of earth-based spirituality, who joyously embrace all of these changes.

The four seasons of light represent the four-fold material manifestations of Spirit affecting and transforming matter. The magick performed during this mystery cycle reveals the nature of the material manifestations or outer translations of the world, and its profound inner meaningfulness as realized by the practicing magician. The completion of an annual cycle represents the natal anniversary of the practitioner, and another milestone in one's life cycle and initiatory process.

10.3 Mystery of Life, Death and Rebirth

The Chthonic mystery concerns itself with the apparent cycle of birth, death and rebirth that affects the vegetation of the earth. Like the Solar mystery, there are four events that denote the center, or maximum power and effectiveness of each season; these events present the mystery of the life-cycle of plants and all living things that derive their life from them, either directly or indirectly.

All living things emulate this life cycle, although at different rates of time. All living things are born at some point, and some time later, die. Life and death are the cycles of living things, and nothing ever seems to escape it. To live is essentially to die. Death seems to be a taboo subject for self-aware living beings who realize that they are fated to die. An awareness of death requires some kind of counter perspective to deal with it and its stultifying powers over the joys of life.

Throughout time humanity has created myths and symbols that allowed it to lessen the overwhelming fear and awareness of death. These myths of immortality have created the illusion that death is not final, and that individual consciousness continues after death.

Christianity and Islam have created highly elaborate myths about the human soul and the survival of death, but many other religions also have some form of this mythology operating in the core of their beliefs. Experience and scientific knowledge has shown how unique each individual human is, and how all are determined by genetics and temporal (environmental) influences. That we are genetically and temporally unique, as is all life, makes our duplication impossible.

The individual survival of death is impossible, since corporeal beings are unique and unrepeatable phenomena. In contrast, Spirit appears to be non-dual, eternal, and therefore, immortal. Through our experience of Spirit, we know all too well the limitations of our existence.

Religious experiences and occult research have shown that the spiritual dimension of consciousness does in fact survive death, but in a manner that is radically different than what is purported in the immortality myths of western religions. What survives is what is left after one eliminates everything associated with the body. This includes all aspects of the self that are based on the body or the mind. Nothing of the individual self survives death except the spiritual dimension of that self.

The individual spirit is an illusion perpetuated by the mind and the body. A person's spiritual essence would be subsumed into the whole of Spirit after death. The individual being completely dies, but the spirit that held and contained that soul as mind and body would remain forever as a facet of the totality of Spirit.

The vegetative cycle of life, death, and rebirth symbolizes the constancy of the life cycle, but also its variety and constant change. The seasonal rebirth that occurs is not the rebirth of individual lives, but the general rebirth of life. The perennial flower that dies in the autumn does not individually return in the following summer. Even plants that live through the winter eventually die off completely, to be replaced with other flora.

The illusion of the constancy of life is actually the emanation of Spirit that resides behind it, acting as the repository of its depth and collective union. The life that dies in the autumn returns in other forms, never repeating and never really returning as it once was. For life death is final, but for Spirit death is only part of the eternal pattern of change. Life is translated and also transformed.

Translation changes that occur in the life cycle represent the creation and destruction of the various manifestations in the spectrum of life. Transformation is where birth or death changes life in relation to Spirit, where the spiritual process engages itself in life (involution), and departs life (evolution) to rejoin the collective union.

As consciousness shifts into spirit, life is transcended within the awareness of the spiritual dimension of the self. Thus one's spirit allows an individual to experience the transformative process of death while one is still alive. This phenomenon can only be realized by one who has accepted immanent death, ceasing to believe in the delusions of immortality popularly held by the masses.

Magick performed through this periodic mystery awakens the spiritual dimension of the self, accepting the power and finality of physical death. When death becomes one's guide, advisor and greatest teacher, then one has begun the proper realization of this mystery.

Conclusion: Four Mysteries

The mysteries of the Moon, the Sun and the Life Cycle are based in the cycle of light and darkness that pervades everything, acting through the diurnal cycle of night and day. Therefore, these four mysteries are tightly related and do not exist in isolation, but as part of a greater spiritual discipline and practice. In this, each of these mysteries becomes fully realized and actualized in the self.

The following is a table that represents the four mysteries and how they relate to each other. Knowledge of this relationship allows one to understand their underlying pattern, which is a variation on the number four.

The Four Mysteries of the Earth

Diurnal Cycle	Lunar Cycle	Solar Cycle	Chthonic Life Cycle
Midnight	New Moon	Winter Solstice	Birth (Candlemas)
Dawn	First Quarter	Spring Equinox	Youth (Beltain)
Noon	Full Moon	Summer Solstice	Maturity (Lammas)
Dusk	Last Quarter	Autumn Equinox	Death (Samhain)

The four mysteries of the earth represent the cycles of change, where that change is realized as a translation or a transformation, or both simultaneously. All of these changes are defined as changes in light and darkness causing inward and outward projections, expressed as life or death.

The key to these mysteries is to master the cycles of light and darkness, both within and without one's self and to realize and embrace death as an integral transformation of life. The key is realized in the union of spirit and life, and how that union affects the individual.

10.4 Mystery of Initiation & Self Transformation

The mystery of initiation and self transformation is based upon the chthonic life cycle and how it relates to the individual who is living and not yet at the point of experiencing death. In life, there are moments when consciousness appears to cease such as during sleep, orgasm, and physical trauma (brain damage or pain avoidance). These moments of the cessation of consciousness are known as the little deaths that break up the continuity of the self immersed in conscious existence.

However, there is also another process where the darkness of the unconscious mind and the light of the conscious mind merge and become one, at that moment of union when conscious transformation is experienced. That process is called transformative initiation. Conscious transformation emulates or symbolizes the cycle of life to death, and from death, rebirth. It is the process whereby the self is disintegrated and reintegrated at a higher and more evolved conscious state of mind. In this, the self is individuated, and then transcended altogether.

The cycle of darkness and light for the individual self is the process of self transformation, where the self becomes aware of death and also the spiritual dimension of the self. The symbolic archetype for this cycle of transformation is the underworld journey, where the hero or heroine undergoes the trials of death and the supreme ordeal, which is spiritual union. Through this union one is able to redefine and reconstitute self- definition.

Ultimately, the transformation of the self causes self-transcendence. A new construct of the trans-personal, trans-egoic and non-dual self becomes an expression or personal extension of Deity within Spirit.

The final transformation of the individual is where an individual becomes one with the Deity and ceases to be an ego based being altogether. However, there are gradations of this achievement, where each level represents a certain point on the spiral of conscious development. These could be called initiatory degrees.

Magickal rituals that embody this mystery are the various initiation rites or major ritual workings of personal transformation (magickal ordeals). All these rites use the double gateway consisting of the western gate of the underworld and the eastern gate of the rebirth of light - the ascendant dawn. The passage through this double gateway is represented by the hero's journey, and the twenty-two stages that are passed through to fulfill the mystery and achieve the integration of consciousness.

10.5 Mystery of Deity and Spirit

The fifth and final mystery is the Mystery of Deity and the personification of that Deity, or its innate manifestation as indivisible Spirit. There is the paradox of whether Deity can or can't be defined in a strict manner through doctrine and dogma since it's always part of the Unity of all Being.

Between religious people, there has often been the intense discussion about whether one's religious definition of Deity should prevail over another person's definition. Spiritual and occult experiences have shown that a specific definition of Deity is impossible to prove, since there can always be a logical argument both for and against that definition as being true. However, ethnocentric opinions about religion and the nature of Deity have persisted.

Religious doctrine and dogma have always relied on belief to bolster its claims for absolute truth. Certainly if one definition for God were absolutely true, then others would have to be false. This, of course, is quite absurd, and represents perhaps the greatest mystery and paradox that faces mankind, and also its greatest crisis.

The paradox is that all definitions of Deity are true as far as they go, and also false, since any definition would be able to be logically refuted. It would seem that the only definition that would be unassailable is that Deity can't be defined per-se, or that all definitions are partially correct since they only define a small part or facet of Deity. The greater part of Deity must therefore be the domain of Spirit itself, the unity of all being; and being a union, it must, by definition, be greater than the sum of all its parts. Deity is a facet of Spirit, and Spirit is formless in its fusion of the All.

Spirit is defined as the unified field of all being, encompassing all things of the living body, the mind and the individual spirit. Spirit is found in the integral expression of living beings, and that expression is ever changing and dynamic; it is eternal in its continuity and infinite in its variations.

Human nature perceives Spirit in a myriad of forms. All forms are true, but also not true, since they are limited. This is the paradox of the nature of Deity, it exists and also doesn't exist as we perceive it.

We personify Deity, and it responds to us, but behind it is the ground base of Spirit, which has neither definition nor any personality. We may perceive spirits embedding all things. We could see angels, demons, elementals, faeries, anonymous spirits, ghosts, demi-gods, saints and masters, and various gods and goddesses. They would all exist as we experience them and more, and also they would be mere illusions. Our assumption that they are real would be correct, but also incorrect, since any definition would be inadequate to define Spirit in its totality.

We may personify Deity as a specific entity or entities; we could function as monotheists, polytheists, or even animists, and we would still only realize part of the puzzle. We could even perceive Deity as being a universal archetype, and we might be getting closer to the truth, but still fail to define either Deity or Spirit fully.

Deity is actually indivisible from Spirit, and they are truly one and the same. It is human nature to see Deity as having a specific personality or individuality, when everything within Spirit is one and has no individuality. When we shed our prejudicial notions about Deity and seek to leave it undefined as a formless manifestation of Spirit, then we begin to approach the truth.

All efforts to define or limit Deity fail when people seek to realize Deity in their minds or through belief and doctrine. The mind can't grasp spirit, and words fail to define something that is inexplicable.

What remains after the elimination of logic, words, doctrine, ideals and dogma/belief is just the experience of Deity and Spirit. It is through experience that Deity is known. But one can never define that experience or build a logical case for truth out of it since it is subjective. Spiritual truths can only be verified by others who have learned to master the process that opens up Spirit to human awareness.

The process that reveals the domain of Spirit to human inquiry involves the adoption of an altered state of consciousness within sacred space. The tools used may include meditation, ritual enactment and contemplation. The mystery of Deity for humanity is to discover, awaken and realize the divinity within oneself.

In ritual magick, and in other disciplines, there are four mechanisms for realizing Deity. These are devotion, invocation, communion and assumption.

Devotion - Deity as Other Approached Through Love

Perhaps the least valued technique in apprehending Deity is through devotion, since it seems so obvious and simple. Some might consider this an archaic practice, since if one perceives Deity operating within oneself, then devotion to it seems not only illogical, but even a form of idolatry.

Perceiving Deity as separate from oneself is not necessarily a sign of being unenlightened, for the greatest saints and sages have seen their relationship to Deity as one of lover to beloved.

We could even say that Deity and humanity are divided for the sake of union, so that they may find a way to unite and become one.[31] This separation of Deity and self is embedded in the reality of the separate self, which was required to ensure the survival of the human species. When we begin to develop and consciously grow and evolve, we start at the same place, which is at the mental egoic level of conscious development.

Once we pass from that starting point, then we progress to the next stage, which is the Centauric level of development, where the separate self is celebrated and even lionized. Devotion to Deity, or Bhakhti, as it is known in the east, deflects the power of Spirit from the petty ego, and instead invests it in a divine other, which eventually becomes revealed as one's immutable higher self.

The practice of spiritual devotion then leads to the next stage, which is the invocation of deity.

Invocation of Deity

The spiritual seeker carefully defines the Deity so that it has a specific personality and character. This definition becomes so real that it creates a vehicle for Deity to connect and commune with the seeker. The more detail that this Deity possesses, the greater capability the seeker has of apprehending and joining with that Deity.

Such a mechanism becomes a bridge between the truly formless Deity within Spirit and one's distinct concept of Deity. The trick of this operation is that seekers must not be too set in their definition of Deity, knowing that it servers a purpose only, and can

---

[31] The seeker achieves union with the Deity through the mystery of the Hierogamos, or Sacred Marriage, which is the core mystery of the Cycle of the Hero - the transformative initiation cycle.

be effectively replaced with any other definition. This definition is a device that magicians call an Eidolon or Imago[32] of God, depending on whether one uses a descriptive device or an actual surrogate.

The successful invocation of the deity causes that entity to appear in one form or another. The devotee then seeks a communal union with it, which leads to the next stage.

Communion with Deity

This operation is the sacralization of the material world by an infusion of Spirit, as accomplished through the active imago or eidolon of the Deity.

Communion is a process of determining spiritual union through assimilation. The imago or eidolon of the Deity blesses substances with its essential self, and thus imbued, these substances are taken internally in some manner by the devotees, who believe that they are joining themselves in a physical way to their imago of Deity.

Communion forges a physical bridge between the seeker and Spirit, through the artifice of the Deity and sacraments. Sacraments can be food and drink, oils, balms, spiritual healing medicines, elixirs, or any inanimate object. Substances become imbued with the numen of the Deity and enter into human life, thus imparting a sacramentation to life itself.

In addition, there are the rituals and blessing of the Deity that marks the passage of life. These are: sacraments of baptism; naming or seining (birth); confirmation (assumption of one's role within a spiritual community); marriage (union of opposites); seniority (retirement); and the final blessing of extreme unction or last rites (death). There is also the sacrament of transformative initiation itself (initiation degrees or holy orders), and is marked by the sacrament of the chrism (oil of anointing), pneuma (breath) and the laying on of hands or the body. Lastly, there is atonement, which represents the process of self-purification, ego abasement and a psychic

---

[32] *Imago* (pl. *Imagines*) in ritual magickal practice is the image or qualities of a spirit o Deity, usually in the form of a descriptive invocation. Eidolon is usually a statue or an individual impersonating a spirit or Deity. Often the statue has been consecrated and charged, with the spirit said to abide within it, and a person wearing a disguise is in deep trance, representing a surrogate for the actual Deity. The surrogate can also be th Priest/ess.

reduction of the ego (simplicity) required to enter into a state of communion with the Deity.

Communion offers the devotee actual contact with the deity. This is sufficient for some, but for others, there is the possibility of immersion and true union, which brings us to the final state, which is the assumption of deity.

Assumption of Deity

This operation is where the seeker, through meditation and deep trance and the use of an imago, becomes the eidolon of the Deity Within.

This is a rite of merging the spirit of the individual with the totality of Spirit, as determined by the imago of the Deity. As one's definition of Deity expands and evolves, becoming completely transcendent, then the operation of assumption fosters a greater awareness of Deity and Spirit within oneself.

This operation ultimately allows one to transcend all definitions of spirit, deity and the self. Assumption is the ultimate ritual vehicle of obtaining true union with Spirit, and is particularly practiced in most earth-base spiritual systems. When assumption becomes the central rite of a religion, it is an obvious indicator that such a religion is immanent in its perspective.

10.6 Ritual Components of the Mysteries

The rituals that are used to activate the five mysteries are an essential part of the grimoire of the magician, witch or neopagan. Magicians who have adopted the basic regimen, and who practices the liturgy of the new earth-based spiritual tradition, have in their repertoire of rituals the meditation session and the circle consecration rite.

The fundamental base for the revelation of the mysteries is the adoption of the proper altered mental state realized within the domain of sacred space. In addition to that, the ritual magician uses the ritual that generates the magnetic or feminine vortex combined with the enactment of the sacred gateway of the West or East to establish the transformative field of the mystery. Within that mystery field, the ritual enactment or meditation of the specific mystery is performed, which activates the mystery process.

Activation causes a powerful transformation to occur in the celebrant, as well as participants. But the key is the apprehension of the mystery's paradox and the impact of its full realization. Blindly performing the rite does not guarantee that the magician will glean the results.

Once the magician successfully turns the key of the specific mystery, then its powers and potencies are unlocked, and the magician undergoes an ordeal, which is the resolution of the activated internal transformation and quiescence of the accompanied psychic trauma.

A series of these ordeals, calculated to challenge the magician at strategic points in one's path, and enacted within all of the five mysteries successively represents the totality of the spiritual and magickal discipline of the initiate.

Practicing magicians will need to establish two notebooks to complete their assembled grimoire. The first is the Book of Lunar Mysteries, and the second is the Book of Solar and Chthonic Seasonal Mysteries. These books will be based on notes and research about the folklore and associated beliefs and practices for the lunar cycles, seasonal full moons and the solar festivals. The greater the amount of material and research that is put into these books, the more powerful the resultant mystery workings will be. These books should be a continuous work in progress, with new and deeper material added to them over time.

An individual or group may also develop separate circle consecration rites for the Lunar and Solar Mysteries, as well as differentiating the Rose Ankh vortex rite. The Solar Sabbats may actually use the Rose Cross device to create a vortex instead of the Rose Ankh. The Chthonic Sabbats, when practiced in group, could even have someone not only assume the role of the Chthonic Godhead, but if at all possible wear a costume and makeup to look like that Deity.

Aspects of the Deity must be developed in great detail so that they have an accessible character. An image, imago or eidolon should be developed for each Deity used in the group's magick, and a Book of Gods and Goddess also developed. The primary Deities used by the individual or group could even have statues and shrines devoted to them. The greater the detail, the more accessible the Deity, and the more one is able to establish an alignment with it. Remember that the chosen Deity is just a place marker for something that is actually unknowable, inexplicable, and wholly of Spirit.

The chthonic solar mysteries may also have corroborating mysteries in association with the stages of human existence, most notably, birth, puberty, maturity and death. The ritual pattern for the chthonic solar mystery can be used in a shortened form (omitting the godhead assumption and magickal working) to facilitate sharing the mysteries within the spiritual community. The chthonic mystery in this rite then becomes one of the mysteries of the human life cycle of seining or naming, hand-fasting, dedication or void filling, consecration (recognition of clergy), eldering (grandfather/mother acknowledgment), and the last rites, or celebration of the entry into the Elysian fields. These rites become the mysteries of the life cycle as shared within the sacralized community.

Epilogue: Mastering the Foundation

Congratulations! You have achieved a wonderful milestone in completing the reading and study of this book.

In the *Disciple's Guide to Ritual Magick*, you were given a complete system and a grimoire that contained the basic components for what I consider to be a beginning system of ritual magick.

Now, we have covered all of the materials in Mastering the Art of Ritual Magick to build a strong foundation for an intermediate level of practice.

By adopting the discipline of ritual magick and faithfully performing the rituals. You are now armed with both experience and a greater depth of knowledge, so you may now proceed with the next level.

It is necessary to recap this material before moving forward to fully comprehend the components of an intermediate system of ritual magick.

Our foundation contained the following topics:

* Four Elements and the Divine Tetrad
* Magickal Concepts of Power
* Magickal Identity
* Techniques of Mind Control
* Magickal Topology (Sacred Space)
* Magickal Ritual Structures
* Performance of Ritual
* Transformative Initiation
* Five Mysteries

Having presented this material in great depth, we have established the proper foundation for a continuation of the magickal work, which is the building of a grimoire of magickal rituals that utilize this foundation as its base.

This is the next objective for this work, and so other books will follow this one. We will need to present the rituals in a new grimoire, but in such a fashion that they will be able to be easily rewritten into a set of personal rituals – to be used in a more advanced magickal system. Of course, you will also need to know how to rewrite these rituals and how to build either a personal magickal discipline for yourself, or for a group, since this system of magick will lend itself to group work as well as solitaire work. In addition to a grimoire, you will also need to forge a magickal key, consisting of tables of correspondences and other materials that will aid in the writing and formulating an intermediate system of ritual magick.

There is a purpose and direction for this series of books and levels of magickal practice. All of this material allows you to gradually master a discipline and practice of ritual magick that will prepare you for the truly greater challenge, the many rituals and practices of the magickal order of the E.S.S.G., also known as the Order of the Gnostic Star. Ultimately, even this material will eventually become published and available to you. The Order has rituals that assist you in mastering the techniques of Elemental Magick, Talismanic Magick, Theurgy, Sacramentation, and even more advanced systems of magick contained in the study and discipline of the magickal system of Archeomancy. In all, there are hundreds of rituals waiting patiently for a group of students like you to study and master them. The present work, Mastering the Art of Ritual Magick is the best possible study for you to prepare for the most advanced magickal lore to be found anywhere.

To get a better idea about some of this fantastic lore, and to know more about the Order itself, I eagerly direct you to examine the following web site. I can assure you, that you'll not be disappointed.

http://www.gnosticstar.org

Your Not So Humble Servant:
Frater Barrabbas Tiresius

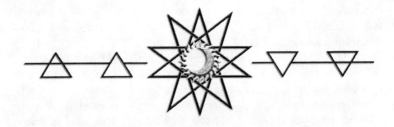

Appendix 1: About Franz Bardon

I consider Bardon to be one of the most important magicians and occultists of the twentieth century. Unfortunately, in occult circles he is far less known than others of his time, such as Israel Regardie, William Grey, Dion Fortune, or even Aleister Crowley. This may be due to the fact that only three books were published by Bardon, and they in turn were translated from the German language to English well after his death.

Bardon was born in Opava, Czechoslovakia, on December 1, 1909.[33] In the late twenties and thirties, Bardon made his living as a stage magician, working under the name of Frabato the Magician. A semi-autobiographical book, called *Frabato the Magician*, outlined the seemingly incredible historical facts of Bardon's life, or at least the facts as presented by his devoted friend and secretary, Otti Votavova. Much of this story is probably fiction mixed with some facts, and clearly there is little of the historical Bardon left for any kind of analysis.

What is known is that Bardon was an exceptional and avid occult student his entire life, and even his avocation as stage magician was tied into his occult studies and practices. Bardon was arrested by the Nazis sometime in 1944, and rescued from a concentration camp somewhere in Eastern Europe by Russian soldiers. He returned to Czechoslovakia after the war, and began to write down his teachings during the 1950's.

He wrote two outstanding works, *Initiation into Hermetics*, and *Magical Evocation*. His third book, *The Key to the True Quabbalah* was less impressive than the previous two, and the work, *Frabato the Magician*, was never published during his life time, and was actually

---

[33] See the website for Bardon's online Biography -
http://www.merkurpublishing.com/franz_bardon_bio.htm

produced from various notes and papers assembled by his secretary. Many consider the fourth book to be incomplete at best, a forgery or fiction at worst.

Looking at pictures of Bardon from his stage magician days and comparing them to pictures of him after the war, it's easy to see that his tenure in a Nazi concentration camp aged him considerably, and probably helped shorten his life. Bardon was arrested by the Czech communist authorities in 1958 during one of the many political purges of that time, and supposedly died of pancreatitis on July 10 at a prison hospital in Brno, at the age of 49. It seems less obvious today in the post cold-war era, but that Bardon may have been arrested because of his published works, illicit occult activities and controversial healing treatments. These activities would have been viewed with great disdain and suspicion by his Stalinist superiors.

What has survived of Bardon's work speaks more about this man than any biographical story, because both of his first two books are neatly laid out in a sequential step by step manner, with theoretical lessons and practical exercises for each step. We will concern ourselves with a few sections of Bardon's first work, *Initiation into Hermetics*, since it has the mind control exercises that are relevant to this work.

Bardon emphasized practical experience over merely theorizing, and believed that the best test of any system was to try it and see how it works. The system that Bardon presents, although perhaps having multiple sources as well as much creative invention, is one that he himself had used and thoroughly worked out in all its details. He makes numerous comments about having personally done this experiment or that as part of the narrative commentary throughout these two books. It is obvious that Bardon was a practicing occultist and magician, and he understood his craft well enough to present a complete training program for individuals who lack a teacher or an organization to initiate and train them.

In Bardon's work one can find material that has its sources in German Theosophy and practical occultism from that fertile period before the war. There are also other sources as well, such as the magickal and mystical lore of Tibetan Buddhism, which he gathered from the voluminous writings of Alexandria David-Neel. Bardon also borrowed from other classic works, such as those by Agrippa, Barrett, and German translations of the *Key of Solomon* and other grimoires available at the time.

Bardon claimed to have no connection with any recognized occult organization and seems to be self taught. Some occultists have speculated that he may have belonged to the Swiss O.T.O., and others have proposed the Fraternity of Saturn. There is no evidence that Bardon belonged to any occult order, and his teachings, although not too exceptional, have the stamp of the self taught, the experimenter and the self initiated. Bardon himself seems to promote self training and self initiation as the best method for gaining occult powers and wisdom, and seems to hold a high degree of disdain for most teachers and occult organizations. If Bardon had belonged to some organization, he would probably have been its greatest advocate and spokesman, and this certainly would have been reflected in his writings in some manner.

In the book *Frabato the Magician*, the main character, Frabato, belongs to a universal secret occult lodge that is only accessible via the akashic plane to high initiates, but this seems more representative of a fictional ideal than of an actual order. So we can conclude that Bardon developed his system of magick, which he called Hermetic, from a long period of research, experimentation and practical work. There is nothing unusual about this phenomenon; it's the typical manner that most systems of magick are created by magicians for their own use.

Magicians have to create their magickal systems because the available collection of practical work and knowledge based upon experience is often severely lacking in books and organizations, and so it must be invented and created by the magician over time. Bardon's system of Hermetic Initiation is one that is very well thought out and organized, showing his genius for practical occult work.

Bardon's concept of the four elements is somewhat unique since he operationally visualizes, and therefore, sees them in a very physical manner. To Bardon, the world is divided into polarities of masculine and feminine energies, although these polarities are in a state of perpetual dynamism and union. The masculine energy on all levels and worlds is Fire, signified by a red color and the qualities associated with electricity. The feminine energy is Water, signified by a blue color and associated with the qualities of magnetism.

The primary polarity is between Fire and Water, representing the sexual polarity of masculine and feminine, and this polarity is the creative and manifesting wave that derived all material, mental and astral things. It is the expression of spirit and deity to be the first fusion of masculine and feminine polarities, and so deity is perceived as a composite like Yin and Yang, symbolized by the Tantric union of God and Goddess. Bardon discusses the necessity of the magician to obtain and emulate this state of perfect union, seeming to imply that perhaps some kind of sex magick is involved. He does not elaborate on any ritualized sexuality in his writings, however, and his practical work is geared toward the solitary individual, as if that represents Bardon's sole domain of expertise.

The Elements of Air and Earth are derived from the primary two elements of Fire and Water, representing two different manifestations of their union. Both of these elements represent some kind of electro-magnetic induction or combination, where Air is fluidic and mercurial, and Earth is static and saturnine.

Human life is defined by Bardon as being tetra-polar, consisting of an interaction of the four Elements and also the Akasha. Balancing the four Elements in the physical body, mind and astral body of the magician was considered the primary objective in Bardon's system of magick. Bardon believed that illnesses of various sorts occurred when the combination of elements in a person became imbalanced, and that healing simply required the body to regain its elemental balance by re-emphasizing the deficient element(s).

In Bardon's system, occultists spend a great deal of time determining their elemental quotient and then achieving balance through the absorption of whatever deficient element. For instance, if someone was very masculine, fiery, emotional and sanguine, then to become more balanced, they would absorb an equal quantity of feminine, magnetic and phlegmatic energies into their physical, mental and astral bodies to become balanced.

Magicians are epitomized by the fact that they are not swayed in any one direction or bias, but can assume any stance, bias or formulation required to achieve and realize their desires in the world. This would be quite a powerful method of controlling the self, and Bardon devotes several chapters of his first book detailing techniques and practices that assist in self mastery. It is also a requirement in this system of magick for the magician to obtain self mastery before attempting to learn the art of invocation and theurgy, and indeed this is a useful guideline in other systems of magick as well.

Bibliography

The following is a list of books that I have assembled for suggested reading for you, the intermediate student. It's necessary for you to be proficient in several disciplines in order to become a master of ritual magick. Therefore, this list will provide you with a brief list of corresponding material that will augment the material presented in the *Mastering the Art of Ritual Magick* series. This list is by no means exhaustive and it represents a selection of books from my own personal library. This list is divided into ten different categories, covering the topics that I felt were vital to the study of advanced ritual magick. These categories are Alchemy, Astrology, Fiction (Occult), Gnosis, Magick, Mythology, Psychology, Qabbalah, Sexuality, Tarot and Wicca & Neopaganism.

Note: Some of these books are quite dated, but there are new and revised versions of them out on the market, and they can be considered of such value as to be indispensable. Also, some of the older books are available free from online distributors in the form of ebooks.

Alchemy

Gilchrist, Cherry, *Alchemy - The Great Work* (Aquarian Press, 1984)
Lindsay, Jack, *The Origins of Alchemy in Graeco-Roman Egypt* (Frederick Muller, 1970)
Regardie, Israel, *The Philosopher's Stone* (Llewellyn Publications, 1970)

Astrology

Hand, Robert, *Horoscope Symbols* (Para Research, 1981)

March, Marion D. & McEvers, Joan, *The Only Way to Learn Astrology*, volumes I - III (ACS Publications, Inc.,1982)

Sakoian, Frances & Acker, Louis S., *The Astrologer's Handbook* (Harper & Row, 1973)

Fiction (Occult)

Attanasio, A. A., *Radix* (Bantam Books, 1981)

Blish, James, *Black Easter* (Dell Publishing, 1968)

Hardy, Lyndon, *Master of the Five Magics* (Del Rey Book, Ballintine, 1980)

-- *Secret of the Sixth Magic* (Del Rey Book, Ballintine, 1984)

-- *Riddle of the Seventh Magic* (Del Rey Book, Ballintine, 1988)

Kurtz, Katherine & Turner-Harris, Debborah, *The Adept*, books I - III (Ace Books, 1991 - 1993)

Leiber, Fritz, *Our Lady of Darkness* (Berkley Publishing, 1977)

Walton, Evangeline, *Prince of Annwn* (Ballintine Books, 1974)

-- *The Children of Llyr* (Ballintine Books, 1971)

-- *Song of Rhiannon* (Ballintine Books, 1972)

-- *The Island of the Mighty* (Ballintine Books, 1970)

Gnosis

Meyer, Marvin & Smith, Richard (Editors), *Ancient Christian Magic - Coptic Texts of Ritual Power* (Harper San Francisco, 1994)

Pagels, Elaine, *The Gnostic Gospels* (Random House, 1979)

Pétrement, Simone, *A Separate God - The Origins and Teachings of Gnosticism* (Harper Collins, 1984)

Smith, Morton, *Jesus the Magician* (Harper & Row, 1978)

Versluis, Arthur, *Theosophia - Hidden Dimensions of Christianity* (Lindisfarne Press, 1994)

Welburn, Andrew, *Gnosis - Mysteries and Christianity* (BPC Wheaton, Ltd, 1994)

Magick

Bardon, Franz, *Initiation into Hermetics* (Dieter Rüggeburg, 1971)

Butler, W. E., *The Magician - His Training and Work* (Willshire Book Co., 1969)

-- *Apprenticed to Magic & Magic and the Qabalah* (Aquarian Press, 1981)

-- *Practical Magic and the Western Mystery Tradition* (Aquarian Press, 1986)
Crowley, Aleister, *Book 4* (Sangreal, 1972)
-- *Magick in Theory and Practice* (Castle Books, 1991)
Fortune, Dion, *Psychic Self-Defence* (Samuel Weiser, 1977)
Grey, William, *Magickal Ritual Methods* (Samuel Weiser, 1969)
Knight, Gareth, *The Practice of Ritual Magick* (Samuel Weiser, 1979)
O'Keefe, Daniel Lawrence, *Stolen Lightning: The Social Theory of Magic* (Vintage Books, 1982)
Regardie, Israel, *Ceremonial Magic: A Guide to the Mechanism of Ritual* (Aquarian Press, 1980)
-- *Foundations of Practical Magic* (Aquarian Press, 1979)
-- *The Complete Golden Dawn System of Magic* (Falcon Press, 1984)
-- *The Tree of Life - A Study in Magic* (Samuel Weiser, 1972)
Stewart, R. J., *Living Magical Arts* (Blandford Press, 1987)
Versluis, Arthur, *The Philosophy of Magic* (Arkana, 1986)

Mythology

Campbell, Joseph, *The Hero with a Thousand Faces* (Bollingen Press, 1973)
-- *The Masks of God - Primitive Mythology* (Bollingen Press, 1974)
-- *The Masks of God - Oriental Mythology* (Bollingen Press, 1974)
-- *The Masks of God - Occidental Mythology* (Bollingen Press, 1974)
-- *The Masks of God - Creative Mythology* (Bollingen Press, 1974)
Jobes, Gertrude, *Dictionary of Mythology, Folklore and Symbols* (Scarecrow Press, 1962)

Psychology

Jung, Carl G., *Man and His Symbols* (Doubleday & Co., 1964)
-- *Archetypes and the Collective Unconscious* (Bollingen Press, 1975)
-- *Symbols of Transformation* (Bollingen Press, 1976)
Mishlove, Jeffrey, *The Roots of Consciousness* (Random House, 1975)
Ornstein, Robert E., *The Psychology of Consciousness* (Viking Press, 1972)
Ornstein, Robert E. (Editor), *The Nature of Human Consciousness* (Viking Press, 1973)
Woolf, V. Vernon, PhD., *Holodynamics* (Harbinger House, 1990)

Qabbalah

Crowley, Aleister, *The Qabalah of Aleister Crowley* (Samuel Weiser, 1973)
-- *Liber 777* (Level Press, 1970)
-- *777 and Other Qabalistic Writings of Aleister Crowley* (Samuel Weiser, 1994)
Davidson, Gustav, *A Dictionary of Angels* (Free Press, 1971)
Fortune, Dion, *The Mystical Qabalah* (Ernest Benn, 1974)
Grey, William, *The Ladder of Lights* (Helios, 1971)
Halevi, Z'ev ben Shimon, *Psychology and Kabbalah* (Samuel Weiser, 1991)
Knight, Gareth, *A Practical Guide To Qabalistic Symbolism*, Volume I & II (Helios, 1972)
Regardie, Israel, *A Garden of Pomegranates* (Llewellyn Publications, 1970)
-- *The Middle Pillar* (Llewellyn Publications, 1970)
Scholem, Gershom, *Kabbalah* (New American Library, 1974)
Whitcomb, Bill, *The Magician's Companion* (Llewellyn Publications, 1993)

Sexuality

Anand, Margo, *The Art of Sexual Ecstasy* (Jeremy P. Tarcher, Inc., 1989)
-- *The Art of Sexual Magic* (Jeremy P. Tarcher, Inc., 1995)
Douglas, Nik & Slinger, Penny, *Sexual Secrets* (Destiny, 1979)
Kappas, John G., Ph.D., *Your Sexual Personality* (Panorama Publishing Co, 1982)
Kelsey, Morton & Barbara, *Sacrament of Sexuality* (Amity House, 1986)

Tarot & I Ching

Campbell, Joseph & Roberts, Richard, *Tarot Revelations* (Vernal Equinox Press, 1979)
Crowley, Aleister, *The Book of Thoth* (Samuel Weiser, 1972)
Hoeller, Stephan A., *The Royal Road* (Theosophical Publishing House, 1988)
Pollack, Rachel, *Seventy-eight Degrees of Wisdom - A Book of the Tarot*, Parts I & II (Aquarian Press, 1980)

Walker, Barbara G., *The Secrets of the Tarot - Way of the Great Oracle* (Merrill-West, 1989)

Wilhelm, Richard & Baynes, Cary F., *The I Ching or Book of Changes* (Bollingen Press, 1973)

Wicca & Neopaganism

Bolen, Jean Shinoda, M.D., *Goddesses in Everywoman* (Harper Colophon Books, 1984)

Farrar, Janet & Stewart, *Eight Sabbats for Witches* (Robert Hale Ltd., 1981)

-- *The Witches Way* (Robert Hale Ltd., 1981)

Harrison, Michael, *The Roots of Witchcraft* (Citadel Press, 1973)

Godwin, Malcolm, *The Holy Grail - Its Origins, Secrets & Meaning Revealed* (Viking Studio, 1994)

Mathews, John & Green, Marian, *The Grail Seekers Companion* (Aquarian Press, 1986)

Patai, Raphael, *The Hebrew Goddess* (Wayne State University Press, 1990)

Stone, Merlin, *When God was a Woman* (Dorset Press, 1976)

Valiente, Doreen, *Witchcraft For Tomorrow* (Robert Hale Ltd, 1978)

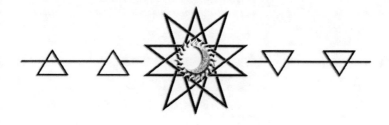

About the Author

Frater Barrabbas Tiresius is a practicing ritual magician who has studied magick and the occult for over thirty-five years. He has emphasized pragmatism, experimentalism and structuralism in a discipline that he believes has become stale and overly conservative. He believes that ritual magick is an art whose mystery is unlocked by continual practice and by personal occult experiences and revelations. He has published his first book "Disciple's Guide to Ritual Magick" in May 2007, published an anthology article "Magic and the Eucharistic Mass" in November 2008, and is in the final editing stages of a new trilogy entitled "Mastering the Art of Ritual Magick", the first volume of which is the present work.

The Trilogy "Mastering the Art of Ritual Magick" begins where the "Disciple's Guide" ends, and attempts to assist intermediate students in building their own personal magickal system. Frater Barrabbas believes that only by building a personal system of magick can a magician ever expect to truly master the art of ritual magick. This is a new grimoire for a New Age – an age of Integral Transformative Ritual Magick.

Frater Barrabbas has belonged to several neopagan, Wiccan and occult organizations, but he believes that each student must ultimately find their own path and develop their own individual way of practicing their occult beliefs, religion and magick.

Did You Like What You Read?

LaVergne, TN USA
07 July 2010
188654LV00003B/80/P